I'M A MORMON NOW WHAT?

A GUIDE TO HELP YOU ALONG THE WAY

I'M A MORMON NOW WHAT?

A GUIDE TO HELP YOU
ALONG THE WAY

CARMEN DAVIS

BONNEVILLE BOOKS
SPRINGVILLE, UTAH

ISBN 13: 978-1-59955-470-9

Published by Bonneville Books, an imprint of Cedar Fort, Inc., 2373 W. 700 S., Springville, UT 84663
Distributed by Cedar Fort, Inc. www.cedarfort.com

LIBRARY OF CONGRESS CATALOGING-IN-PUBLICATION DATA

Davis, Carmen, 1970-
I'm a Mormon, now what? / Carmen Davis.
p. cm.
ISBN 978-1-59955-470-9
1. Mormon converts. 2. New church members--Religious life. 3. Mormons--Social life and customs. 4. Church of Jesus Christ of Latter-day Saints--Membership. I. Title.

BX8638.D38 2010
289.3'32--dc22

2010026875

Cover design by Amy Hackett
Cover design © 2010 by Lyle Mortimer
Edited and typeset by Kelley Konzak

Printed in the United States of America

10 9 8 7 6 5 4 3 2 1

Printed on acid-free paper

To my wonderful husband, Shan, who has always encouraged me to step outside my comfort zone. To my four boys, Kade, Zayne, Owen, and Mason, who make sure that I never get too "comfortable" in any zone, anywhere! To my siblings, who told me to "just write the dang book." Finally, to my amazing parents, Dennis and Mae Dilts, who have spent their lives showing me by example how to live.

Contents

Acknowledgments

This book was the result of hours of discussion with members of the Church in several branches, wards, and stakes in several states and even two different countries, and the influence of many great examples of Latter-day Saints faithfully living the gospel who have touched my life. Thank you to my sisters, who shared openly many of the ideas, thoughts, and opinions used in the final product. To my brother, who has faithfully served in his Church callings and provided an example for my husband and my sons—you're the best, Morg! Thank you to my brothers-in-law, who let us girls sit at the kitchen table on many occasions, laughing as I received "advice" on things not to forget in the book. Thank you to my sister Denise for taking time away from her girls to edit the original work. Thank you to my nieces and nephews who are striving to live the gospel in this crazy world and set a great example for their auntie. Thank you to Auntie Faye and Debbie Hawke, who challenged me to graduate from seminary—even if they had to move the deadline on a couple of occasions. Thank you to my Young Women leaders—especially Ruth Hawke, who showed me by her example the type of person I want to be when I grow up. And last but certainly not least, thank you to the wonderful staff at Cedar Fort, who believed in this project from the start. You guys are amazing!

1 The Journey Begins

Embarking on Your Life as a Member

"If all difficulties were known at the outset of a long journey, most of us would never start out at all."
Dan Rather

Pretend you're going on a trip. You know exactly where you're going and, like most of us, you carefully plan every detail of your journey, chart your course, maybe even pack a road map in the car for the just-in-case moments. You all pile into the car and set off on what you know will be an amazing and wonderful adventure. For the first little bit, you're in your own neighborhood and things look pretty familiar. Neighbors wave to you as you pass, and you're confident that you'll reach your destination safely.

One left turn when you should have made a right, and everything changes. No longer are the neighbors you know waving from the roadsides. The streets no longer look familiar, the road signs aren't what you expect to see, and even though you still have your road map, without knowing where you are there's no way to figure out how to get back on the right path. The longer you're lost, the less confident you feel and the more you begin to doubt your decision to embark on such a journey. Without stopping to get directions and reassurance that you're on the right path and that you can find your way, you may be tempted to stop the journey and just backtrack until you get to where you began. The excited and promising feelings you had when you started are shrinking rapidly, and you're soon left with overwhelming feelings of insecurity, doubt, and dread.

For many of you, this experience may not be something you'll ever experience, and for that, I congratulate you! Being lost is a very unpleasant experience and not one I recommend. Our family happened to have one of these experiences in December 2001.

We had started our journey in our sleepy little town of Eureka, Montana, population about 1,100 (no, that's not a typo). It was the week of Christmas, and we were headed to my sister's wedding at the Los Angeles California Temple. Since purchasing plane tickets for our family of six was financially out of the question, we decided to drive south and make it a Christmas adventure for us all. We—mostly I—had carefully plotted our course, and I was confident in my ability to get us safely to our destination. The first part of the journey was in familiar territory, since I had been a student at BYU and had driven the road from Montana to Provo, Utah, more times than I cared to remember. The boys were excited to be on an adventure. We listened to books on tape, sang Christmas carols, and genuinely enjoyed the trip. After a few stops along the way to sightsee, celebrate Christmas, and get some rest for a day or so, we managed to make it without incident to my sister's soon-to-be in-laws' home in Newbury Park, California.

All the family had arrived, and final preparations for the wedding and the reception were well underway. My husband, who is a contractor, was quickly enlisted to do some repairs on the home where the reception was to take place. With the house in various stages of construction and chaos, those of us with children decided that since we had made it all the way to southern California, leaving California without a trip to Disneyland would be unacceptable. On the morning of December 28, we loaded up and headed out in search of fun and adventure at Disneyland. My husband, who had been the driver on the journey thus far, stayed behind to finish up the various projects at the Hannemann home. My younger brother was acting as my new driver, and I continued to be the navigator, ever confident. Since it was daylight and we were headed to a major tourist destination, the roads were very clearly marked, and we arrived safely at the theme park without a problem. We spent an exhausting, although fun day at Disneyland, and as our little ones began to fall asleep in strollers and on parents' laps, we decided to end our day.

While we were on our fun adventure, those left in Newbury Park decided to find us accommodations in the apartments next to the temple so that we could avoid the travel and traffic in the morning. This sounded like a well-thought-out plan, and since it was less driving in the dark with sleeping children, we were very much in agreement. We headed back to where we had parked our cars and discussed the quickest way to reach the temple on Santa Monica Boulevard. It was now well after dark—almost 11:00 p.m.—and the streetlights didn't give off nearly as much light as the sun had. The driver of the other vehicle in our group had spent the previous night at the temple apartments. He checked the map and had a clear idea of where he was headed. His instructions were clear: pull out of the parking garage, head south on Interstate 5 until you reach California Highway 22, take that west to the 405, go north on Interstate 405 until you reach Santa Monica Boulevard, and turn right. The temple would be on our left.

I'll admit, it sounded idiot proof. We headed to our car, loaded the sleeping children, and exited from the parking garage. As soon as we left the safety of the parking garage, we realized we were in trouble. For those of you who have never been to Disneyland, take a note for yourselves in case you ever visit: There are two parking garages at Disneyland. One is the Disney princesses and the other is Mickey and friends. We were not in the same parking garage as the other vehicle in our group! We pulled out of the garage and saw the signs for I-5, and we thought we were headed in the right direction. As soon as we reached the interstate, we realized that we should have gotten better directions, since we were headed north, not south, on Interstate 5. We began looking for some place where we could turn around, but because we were unfamiliar with the area and it was dark, we couldn't seem to find an exit that looked like it would also be an entrance back onto the interstate, heading south. After several unsuccessful exits from the interstate, we agreed that we'd just continue heading north on I-5 until we saw a road heading to the west. Of course finding a road heading west was no problem, and even though we had no idea where we were, we made a decision and headed west toward our destination.

That is where the lesson on being lost comes in. The road was indeed headed west toward Interstate 405, but it was definitely not the road to take. Somehow we had made some bad decisions and ended up in Compton, California, after midnight on a Friday night. We still had our road map and knew our destination, but without knowing where we were and what to do, those were useless.

We were in extremely unfamiliar territory. Many of the streetlights in the area stood useless beside the road, their bulbs broken. We encountered a police chase, with the police officers in riot gear. We passed vehicles riddled with bullet holes and windows taped up with duct tape. We saw people with guns and drug deals going on right in public. It was truly an experience I'll never forget. The longer we drove, the worse things got. Finally, I convinced my brother that we needed to stop and ask for directions. Because of the area we were in, this was not something he considered a good idea, or even only a mildly bad idea—he thought I was insane. It took a few blocks to find a convenience store that he would stop at, but he refused to get out and ask for directions. So after a quick prayer, I got out of our vehicle and made the trip across the parking lot to the window of the store.

It turned out that after dark in that area, the doors to the convenience stores are locked and the employee sits behind bulletproof glass and takes your order. He then gets the things you are purchasing and opens a drawer, not unlike a drive-up bank teller. You put in your money, and he returns your change and the purchased items to you via the drawer. Not only did I purchase a map, but I also asked the kind fellow working that evening if he could draw on the map the quickest and safest route to our destination. Despite our obvious differences, this employee took the time to help me. He gave us precise, detailed instructions, including landmarks. And by following these instructions carefully and without exception, we found our way to the temple and to the arms of our loving families that night.

Just as the temple was our goal at the beginning of our journey, so should it be the goal of every member of The Church of Jesus Christ of Latter-day Saints. President Gordon B. Hinckley taught, "I believe that no member of the Church has received the ultimate which this Church has to give until he or she has received his or her temple blessings in the house of the Lord."[1]

Taking the missionary discussions, conversion, and baptism are merely the first steps in the eternal progression of new converts. The road they're on is not an easy road. Not that it is super easy for those of us who were raised in member families, but for new converts, it is even more difficult. There is a culture to Mormonism that is not easily understood, and navigating through it is difficult for the tender testimonies of our newest members. In his conference address in April 1999, President Hinckley shared a letter from a new convert in which she wrote:

"My journey into the Church was unique and quite challenging. This past year has been the hardest year that I have ever lived in my life.

It has also been the most rewarding. As a new member, I continue to be challenged every day . . . Church members don't know what it is like to be a new member of the Church. Therefore, it's almost impossible for them to know how to support us."[2]

President Hinckley then admonished us:

"I challenge you, my brothers and sisters, that if you do not know what it is like, you try to imagine what it is like. It can be terribly lonely. It can be disappointing. It can be frightening. We of this Church are far more different from the world than we are prone to think we are."[3]

This woman goes on:

"When we as investigators become members of the Church, we are surprised to discover that we have entered into a completely foreign world, a world that has its own traditions, culture, and language. We discover that there is no one person or no one place of reference that we can turn to for guidance in our trip into this new world. At first the trip is exciting, our mistakes even amusing, then it becomes frustrating and eventually, the frustration turns into anger. And it's at these stages of frustration and anger that we leave. We go back to the world from which we came, where we knew who we were, where we contributed, and where we could speak the language."[4]

It is with that in mind that I hope to provide a place of reference, or a road map, with some loving instructions that will aid our new converts as they travel the exciting yet sometimes frustrating journey as members of The Church of Jesus Christ of Latter-day Saints.

NOTES

1. Gordon B. Hinckley, "Some Thoughts on Temples, Retention of Converts, and Missionary Service," *Ensign*, Nov. 1997, 49.
2. Gordon B. Hinckley, "Find the Lambs, Feed the Sheep," *Ensign*, May 1999, 104.
3. Ibid.
4. Ibid.

2 Every Road Has Construction Zones

The Things They Don't Tell You

"The road to success is always under construction."
Lily Tomlin

My dad is a convert to The Church of Jesus Christ of Latter-day Saints. He's been a member for over forty years—at some times more committed than at others, but always a member and always with a strong testimony. Last Christmas, as we were discussing conversion to the gospel, he expressed the notion that converts have many misconceptions when they join the Church. He affectionately calls these "the things no one tells you." Not that there are big doctrinal secrets anyone is trying to keep from you. Not that anyone is trying to mislead you or deceive you in any way—but there are things you may assume that no one corrects you on. Dad said most of his periods of less activity in the Church were as a result of having to face one of these misconceptions and not knowing how to cope with or endure it. This chapter is for you, Dad!

President Spencer W. Kimball said, "This life, this narrow sphere we call mortality, does not, within the short space of time we are allowed here, give to all of us perfect justice, perfect health, or perfect opportunities."[1]

Joining the Church will be an amazing blessing and help in your life. Unfortunately, things won't always go the way you think they should go as a result. Your life won't instantly become perfect. Things will go wrong. Bad things will happen to you and to people you love. You will continue to have trials, and Satan will still be permitted to tempt you. The spiritual high you felt at your conversion and as a new member will fade. Your prayers won't always be answered the way you want. You'll have to build your own testimony one principle at a time and over years, not seconds. It's not what happens to you as a member of the Church that will make your life great; it's how you choose to use the gospel to overcome and endure those challenges that will make the difference.

What an amazing feeling it is to know The Church of Jesus Christ of Latter-day Saints is true and to have the Holy Spirit testify to you of this truth. You almost feel as though your testimony is invincible! My husband, Shan, calls it being on a "spiritual high." For the first year after his baptism, he felt like that all the time. He remembers it as one of the best times of his life. I know how powerful and almost overwhelming the feeling of the Spirit can be. I can still remember the first time I felt and recognized the Spirit testify to me as I struggled to gain a testimony of the truthfulness of the gospel.

I had just finished studying the Book of Mormon in seminary. I had already successfully completed two years of seminary but had yet to gain my own testimony. As a part of our study that year, we were to read the Book of Mormon on our own—from cover to cover. I had started probably hundreds of times and could quote from memory the first verse: "I, Nephi, having been born of goodly parents . . . ." But, in all my years as a member of the Church, I had never finished the book. I think it was the chapters in 2 Nephi when Nephi quotes Isaiah that lost me every time. That year we had been challenged by our seminary teacher and our Church Education System area representative, Brother Woods, to read the book—not from the last page we had previously read but from the first verse to the final *amen.*

I accepted the challenge and signed a contract with my teacher that I would read it. As the year progressed, it wasn't easy. Those tough chapters in 2 Nephi almost stopped me again, but this time my commitment was greater than my lack of understanding of Isaiah's writings, and I continued. As I neared the end of the Book of Mormon, I came to Moroni 10:4 and read the promise contained there:

"And when ye shall receive these things, I would exhort you that ye would ask God, the Eternal Father, in the name of Christ, if these things are not true; and if ye shall ask with a sincere heart, with real intent, having faith in Christ, he will manifest the truth of it unto you, by the power of the Holy Ghost."

I put down my Book of Mormon, knelt down on the floor beside my bed, and offered up a prayer to my Heavenly Father to know if the book was true. The love I felt as I ended my prayer was almost overwhelming. Without warning, tears began to flow down my cheeks, and I *knew* that the Book of Mormon was true. I knew that I was a child of God and that he loved me. He loved me enough to hear and answer my prayer. Oh, if only I could have made the feeling from that moment last forever!

As I got older and made some serious mistakes in my life, I never doubted that testimony. Even when I was making selfish choices that made it impossible to live the gospel and to feel the Spirit, I knew that I was a beloved daughter of heavenly parents. I also knew that the Church was true, even when I was unwilling to live it. It was right—I was not! It was that testimony that eventually brought me back to the Church. It was also a witness from the Spirit that reassured me when I returned to activity that I was forgiven for my sins—each and every one—and could move on with my life.

The gift of the Holy Ghost you received after your baptism will help you as it did me. It will serve as a guide and provide direction to help you find your way. It will also testify to you of the truthfulness of the doctrines you're learning. It will help you build a testimony of truth. It can also help you work through trials that seem to have no eternal consequences.

Several summers ago our family decided to go on a fishing trip on the Flathead River at the edge of Glacier Park. It was only a day trip from our home, and with four young boys, we were bound to have an adventure. We loaded the family up in the truck as well as our two-year-old black lab, Samson, and started the drive. We had a great day, and the boys caught their limit of fish. When we were ready to head home, we decided to return by a different route. After driving for about half an hour, Shan stopped to get some cold cans of pop out of the cooler in the back of the pickup. Refreshed, we settled in for the rest of the two-hour drive home. As we arrived in the town of Whitefish, Montana, Shan and the boys decided they needed to stop at the sporting goods store to purchase some new fishing lures. I got out to get something cold to drink from the cooler and quickly discovered that Samson was not in the truck. I called his name and searched the parking lot—no dog! When Shan and the boys came out of the store, I told them of our dilemma.

It was near 9:00 p.m. and would be dark within the hour, and the last stop we had made was almost two hours back up the road. Despite the cries of our boys, we decided to finish heading home and look for our dog after church the next day. Before heading to bed that night, our family knelt in prayer, and Zayne pled with Heavenly Father that our dog would be kept safe for the night and that we would find him and bring him home.

Immediately following our church meetings, the boys and I jumped in the truck to begin the search. Shan had priesthood leadership meetings and was unable to join us on our quest. We returned to the Flathead area, backtracking the way we had come the evening before. As we drove, we stopped often to call Samson's name. We stopped at a few homes on the side of the road, but since this area was not well populated and most homes were weekend retreats, Sunday afternoon was not a good time to find many people around. We made one stop at the little community of Polebridge and asked at the general store, post office, gas station, restaurant, hotel, campground, community hall, and anywhere else we could think of. No one had found a dog.

We drove all the way north to our fishing hole from the previous day without any luck. Once there, we searched the woods and the riverbank for about thirty minutes before I informed the boys that we needed to be heading home. It was almost seven by then, and we still had the two-hour drive to get home. As we turned the truck around, the boys asked that we pray one more time for Samson. This time our prayer was different—we prayed that if we could not find him, he would be safe and would find a family that would love him as much as we had.

Back down the road we drove, too upset to do much more than sit in gloomy silence. As we rounded a corner in the gravel road, Kade noticed a small log building, partly hidden in the trees. From the location of the building, it could not be seen heading north. Kade begged me to stop, but I had reached the end of my patience for the day and was ready to end the search, so I drove past. Kade insisted that he knew we needed to go back and that if we did, we would find Samson. Reluctantly, I turned the truck around and into the parking lot of this sad little building.

Nailed to the side of the building near what appeared to be the front door was a little sign that read, "North Flathead Community Hall." It was as dark as a tomb inside the dirty window. I peered inside with disinterest and stepped back. As I returned to the truck, I heard someone whisper, "Look inside the window." I knew I had just looked inside and had not seen a thing, so I ignored the prompting. Down the two rickety steps I went and started across the small patch of grass toward the truck. "Look inside the window," again the whisper came. More annoyed than anything else, I bounded up the steps and pressed my face to the dusty glass.

Inside the window, not five feet from where I had just stood, I could see a chalkboard. Written on the board in scribbled letters was a brief message. "Found black lab—Dan Flemming."[2] That was it—no date, no phone number, nothing else. We headed south toward civilization, and as we neared the sign for the community of Polebridge, again Kade insisted we needed to stop. By the time he had convinced me to go into Polebridge to ask, I had already missed the turn. I slammed the truck into reverse and altered my course.

When we arrived back at the Polebridge Mercantile, no one seemed to know a Dan Flemming. As I turned to leave, a little old man from the back of the store shuffled forward.

"Did ya say Dan Flemming?" he asked. "That's his nephew's truck out in the parking lot. Maybe he'll be able to help ya."

Out the door I went at a dead run as the young boy coaxed the rusty old truck to life. I tapped on the window and asked if his uncle had found a dog.

"Found one last night," the boy replied. "It's a real nice dog. Are ya sure ya want him back?"

I assured him that the boys most definitely did want their dog and friend back. Reluctantly, he agreed to lead us to his uncle's house. As we approached what can only be described as a shack, Samson bounded out the door toward us. He ran right past me and jumped into the cab of the pickup with the boys, as though nothing had happened.

I thanked Mr. Flemming for the care he had given Samson, and after offering him a reward (which he refused), I pulled my tired body back into the truck and began the rest of the drive home.

As we drove, I asked Kade how he had known we needed to stop at that old building and then again at Polebridge. He explained that "sometimes you just get this feeling, and it kind of makes the hair stand up on your neck. That's how you know."

We spent the rest of our drive that Sunday evening singing Primary songs and sharing stories of times we had listened to the promptings of the Holy Ghost. It was a wonderful ending to an experience I hope none of us will ever forget.

I've been fortunate many times throughout my life to have the Spirit as my companion to guide me and testify to me of truths. I have also had times when I've had to muddle through on my own. Those are tough times, but also times of great learning and growth. As you continue to learn and grow in the gospel, you too will have periods of time when you have difficulty feeling the Spirit. That's one of those things no one tells you.

It's hard. It's even a little scary. And those are the times when Satan tempts you the most. Make a commitment to live the gospel completely so you're worthy of the gift of the Holy Ghost. Stay away from people and places that make it difficult for you to hear the still small voice of the Spirit. Wrong choices can leave you alone without the help and guidance you may desperately need at a critical time in your life. It's like having a brand new car in the driveway and no key to start it!

It is during these difficult times that no one tells you about when it will be important for you to stay close to the Church. Attend your meetings, read your scriptures, and pray. Pray to feel the Spirit. Pray to remain strong in the gospel. Pray to increase your testimony. Pray "with a sincere heart, with real intent" (Moroni 10:4) and then listen for the answers, realizing that sometimes the answer will not come when you want it and understanding that sometimes the answer may be "no." Just continue to pray.

Prayer is a powerful tool to help us navigate this mortal world. Like a navigational system in your car that gives you directions once you provide a destination, prayer can give us direction when we open that line of communication. Just as loving parents would not allow their child to leave home without a way to call, our heavenly parents didn't send us here to make it on our own. They provided a way for us to be in constant communication with them—through prayer.

Unlike the calls from our children, who we send out into the world with cell phones or access to email or computer networks, where we can provide an immediate and direct response to their requests for help or answers to their problems, prayer is a practice of patience. It is also dependent on you dialing the number. It's up to you to reach out to your Father in Heaven for the help, blessings, and guidance you seek.

A sad misconception that many members, new and old alike, have is that God will always grant you the things you earnestly and worthily ask for in your prayers. We also incorrectly believe sometimes that not only will we get what we want, but we'll also get it at the time we want it. That would be wonderful, but it's not always going to be that way. As children on this earth, we don't always know what is best for us—in fact, if we're anything like my children, we probably rarely know what is best for us.

My boys all have a bedtime. Even my oldest, who is a junior in high school, has a ten o'clock bedtime. It's a bit of a source of contention in our family since bedtimes change with age. The younger ones always feel their bedtimes are unfair and should be the same as their older brothers'. They come frequently and earnestly begging, pleading, and attempting to justify why a later bedtime would be beneficial for them. Occasionally we relent and let them have what they have begged for, even though we, as parents, know that it is not what is best for them.

Without exception, the next day is miserable. They're tired and cranky and just not a lot of fun to be around. We're annoyed because they're tired, and the day is just a disaster! It's then that we have the opportunity to teach them that sometimes what we want isn't what's best for us.

That's how prayer works. We can beg and plead, and sometimes our Heavenly Father will relent and allow us to have what we've requested. It may not be what's best for us, but it's what we've asked for. More often, though, we will receive the answer that is best at the time that is right—not in our time, but in the Lord's time. This is another one of those things no one tells you.

In times when our prayers are answered in a way that is not what we wanted or when they are not answered in the time we feel they need to be answered, we may experience bitterness, resentment, and anger. It's at these times that we need to continue to exercise our faith in the Lord. It can be difficult, but those members who choose to accept the will of our Father in Heaven and continue in faith are blessed eternally. This truth won't make it easier to bear, but it can give us an eternal perspective and build our faith if we allow it. Pray for what you righteously desire, but also pray to accept the will of the Father and then faithfully follow it. That is where the true blessings lie.

As you continue on your journey, you will meet many wonderful, faithful, spiritual members of the Church. They can offer you help and guidance as you grow in the gospel. As you come to know these wonderful people, you may feel that you're not as strong of a member in the Church as they are. You may doubt that you'll ever be as strong as they are or as knowledgeable about the gospel as they have become. You may even have times when you're jealous of their testimonies and wish that you could share what they have. It's another one of those new-member secrets.

Part of coming to this life on earth is to grow, progress, and prove ourselves. Each of us must work to progress to our fullest capacities. In order to do that, we must all gain our own testimonies of gospel truths and principles. It cannot be, and we should not want it to be, any other way. What we become will be a reflection of our dedication, learning experiences, hard work, and efforts. You can become someone to look up to.

I'm a fairly aggressive driver. My husband constantly gives me trouble about the way I drive. Despite the sad fact that I spend the summer months driving too fast, I have only gotten two speeding tickets in the twenty-four years I've been driving. Don't misunderstand—I know that speeding is wrong. It's against the law and dangerous too. I've only gotten two tickets, but I've deserved many more. I've been pulled over for speeding more times than I'd like to admit.

Over time and through my experiences, I've developed a testimony that speeding will result in getting a ticket and having to pay the consequences of your actions. You might not get caught every time, but eventually you will be accountable for your choices. I've had to pay fines, and I know that's how the principle works: you speed, you get caught, you pay for your choices. No matter how strong my testimony of that principle is or how many times I share that testimony, I can't give it to someone else. Everyone has to develop a testimony of that principle for himself.

In the summer of 2009, my oldest, Kade, got his driver's license. He has spent sixteen years of his life riding in the car with me—watching me drive and develop my testimony of the law of speeding. Unfortunately, he has watched me create bad habits and make bad choices and not get caught. He has been with me a number of times when I have been pulled over for speeding. He has seen me deal with the consequences of my actions as I've driven to the county offices to pay my fine. He has also heard me testify to him on numerous occasions about the dangers of speeding and the importance of obeying the laws of the roads. As much as I would love for him to share my testimony or to learn from my experiences about following the speed limits, he cannot automatically know and feel what I do. He'll have to learn that principle for himself. It may be a costly lesson and may take him a long time to develop a testimony of it, but the lesson will be learned, and the testimony will be developed.

The same is true with gospel principles. As much as you may want to build your testimony from others' learning and experiences, it's not possible. You will strengthen your testimony only through your own trials, experiences, study, and faith. That's an essential part of the eternal plan—and really not as much of a secret as you might think!

Another misconception of many members of the Church, old and new alike, is that once a principle has been learned and a testimony built on that doctrine, you never have to go back and learn that again. Wrong! As we go through life, we have periods where certain gospel principles are more pertinent to the issues we're dealing with at that time. As time passes and we don't use that principle or focus on it, our testimony of it can weaken, and we forget what we've learned. It's not until we have a crisis that requires us to reconcentrate on that certain principle that we realize our testimony of it may have been weakened and we have to relearn what we thought we already knew. It can be frustrating at times, but each time we relearn or recommit to a gospel principle, it becomes a more significant part of our lives and a mightier force to help us in the long run.

Most of us know when something is hot. If you're at all like me, you've burned yourself enough to realize that heat can hurt. Even though I know the fireplace is hot and that if I'm not careful, I can get burned, sometimes I open the doors to it without taking the necessary measures to make sure I'm safe. I usually grab the handles carefully and loosely at first, testing the heat. If I'm in a hurry or don't want to take the time to find a pot holder or rag of some kind to protect me from the heat, I'll foolishly grab onto the handles and try to open the doors without getting burned. I know that I'll get burned. It's happened a lot, but I seem to forget or get lazy, and at times I'm willing to risk the pain. Sometimes, however, the heat doesn't seem as intense as before, and I gamble that I can do what I need to do without the safeguard of the pot holder. Inevitably, I'm rushing to the nearest sink to rinse my burned fingers under some cold water. The principle has never changed; I have just become lazy or forgetful and need to relearn an important lesson that keeps me safe.

That's sometimes how your membership will be. You'll get lazy or forgetful. You may even think you can make choices that are contrary to gospel principles without getting hurt, but you can't. Just like the law of heat, the gospel principles will not change. It's up to you to keep on living them and building your testimony of their truth throughout your life.

Perhaps the biggest misconception for new members is that now that you have joined the Church, your life will be perfect. Life is a difficult journey for most of us, not an uneventful stroll in the park. There will be many trials that come our way, regardless of how we are living our lives or how diligent we are in keeping the commandments.

Elder Jeffrey R. Holland said:

> We will face things we do not want to face for reasons that may not be our fault. Indeed, we may face difficult circumstances for reasons that were absolutely right and proper, reasons that came *because* we were trying to keep the commandments of the Lord. . . .
>
> . . . Everyone, including, and perhaps especially, the righteous, will be called upon to face trying times. . . .
>
> . . . We need to realize that just because difficult things happen, it does not mean that we are unrighteous or that we are unworthy of blessings or that God is disappointed in us.[3]

My husband and I were married in a civil ceremony in Las Vegas in 1993. After five years of marriage, Shan joined the Church, and we had the privilege of being sealed in the Cardston Alberta Temple in October 1998. It was an absolutely wonderful day and an incredibly spiritual experience. I can quite honestly say I loved him more the moment we joined hands across the altar in the temple than I had at any time in our relationship, including when we were first dating and were "so in love!" We had worked hard, and he had made some huge changes and sacrifices in his life in order for us to be an eternal family. I could not have been happier.

When we left the temple that day, I was positive that our little family would be perfect. Trials and troubles we had experienced in the past would no longer be a problem for us. I was devastated when, as the days passed, our family still had many of the same problems we had before we were sealed in the temple. My two-year-old still cried when I took him to nursery on Sunday. My five-year-old still refused to wear the clothes I set out for him. And my husband and I still had the occasional argument. I was positive that none of that was supposed to happen to an eternal family. I'll admit there were days when I didn't want to spend the next ten minutes with them, never mind eternity. What was wrong? We were supposed to be perfect!

What I had failed to realize is that perfect people get translated; imperfect people get to stay on earth and be tested and learn. Obviously my family has a lot of learning to do because none of us has been translated yet and we still have problems, now having more to do with wanting to use the family car than choosing what to wear or whether to go to nursery. Our temple sealing didn't erase our faults, it just gave us the ability, encouragement, and inspiration to look at life with an eternal frame of reference rather than an earthly frame.

Little things like dirty socks left on the floor or tucked into the couch cushions (thanks Zayne) lose importance when compared to eternal principles. Don't get me wrong—the dirty socks still drive me crazy, but I try not to make such a big deal out of them. It's learning to apply a new perspective to the everyday problems that will help you overcome challenges. The challenges will continue to come. Your baptism didn't entitle you to a free pass through life.

There may be problems in your life that are way above and beyond the everyday variety. So often we hear people ask why bad things happen to good people and complain about how life doesn't seem fair. In many cases these people are probably right: life isn't fair. Life itself is not the reward—it is the test. Life is filled with hard choices, trials, sorrow, and pain. Life is sometimes filled with wayward children, the loss of loved ones, financial difficulties—the list goes on and on. No matter what you're challenged with, it's almost certain that someone somewhere is suffering or has suffered a trial similar to yours. It's how you act in the face of your adversities that will contribute to your end reward.

Elder Dieter F. Uchtdorf said, "Enduring to the end is not just a matter of passively tolerating life's difficult circumstances or 'hanging in there.' Ours is an active religion, helping God's children along the strait and narrow path to develop their full potential during this life and return to Him one day. Viewed from this perspective, enduring to the end is exalting and glorious, not grim and gloomy. This is a joyful religion, one of hope, strength, and deliverance."[4]

I have a good friend who is a faithful member of the Church. As long as I've known her, she has strived to live the gospel and fulfill her callings in the Church willingly, and in my opinion she's amazing at everything she does. She married in the temple to a wonderful man and was blessed with four beautiful daughters. Her family could have been a poster for amazing LDS families.

In the spring of 2008, tragedy struck her family. Her husband, oldest daughter, and third little one were killed in a bizarre yet devastating automobile accident. The other passenger in the vehicle, her seven-year-old daughter, was rushed to the hospital and placed on life support. Her precious little spirit hovered near death for weeks. This faithful sister left her daughter's bedside only long enough to bury her husband and other babies.

She sat by her daughter's hospital bed and prayed for her recovery, but in her hospital blogs she wrote of her willingness to accept the Lord's will. It was during this time in the hospital that she noticed a lump in her neck. One day while the doctor was examining her daughter, this sister asked the doctor to take a look at the lump. She was immediately rushed to an oncologist, where she was diagnosed with cancer. She underwent chemotherapy and radiation to treat the cancer. She lost her hair and most of her energy but none of her beauty or faith!

Throughout her ordeal, this amazing sister remained positive. The messages she posted on her blog provided many of us with inspiration and motivation to overcome the small trials and hurdles that were in our paths as we watched her remain faithful through seemingly insurmountable suffering. Never have I seen my friend or even a photo of her when she does not have a smile on her beautiful face. She has endured our Father in Heaven's will without anger, resentment, or bitterness. She gave uplifting hope to all of us with her words:

"Although I was experiencing great trial and sorrow, [Heavenly Father] did not leave me alone to endure the unimaginable pain that I was being filled with. I had a choice to make. I could be bitter and angry, or better and sanctified."[5]

She is my modern-day example of the Bible's Job, who said, "For I know that my redeemer liveth, and that he shall stand at the latter day upon the earth" (Job 19:25).

My friend continues to inspire me to press forward with a happy heart, a willing spirit, and a sure knowledge that although bad—

sometimes horrible—things happen, we can find comfort in our membership in this wonderful Church as we rejoice in the gospel.

No matter how long you have been a member of the Church, how strong your testimony is, or how much knowledge you have of gospel principles, you will have times of sorrow, trial, and tribulation. It's part of all our lives, even members of the Church. Good people get sick; loved ones pass away; children fall away from the gospel; temple marriages do sometimes end in divorce. As much as our Heavenly Father would love to remove these experiences from our lives in order to spare us pain and sorrow, he loves us enough to allow us to have these experiences so we may have the possibility to learn, grow, and return to him again someday. That's the one thing that everyone *should* tell you, but somehow no one ever does.

NOTES

1. Spencer W. Kimball, "The Abundant Life," *Ensign*, Oct. 1985, 3.
2. The name has been changed because I am horrible at writing in my journal and can't remember eight years later what that kind man's name was.
3. Jeffrey R. Holland, "Lessons from Liberty Jail," CES Fireside for Young Adults, September 7, 2008, Brigham Young University (Salt Lake City: Intellectual Reserve, 2008).
4. Dieter F. Uchtdorf, "Have We Not Reason to Rejoice?," *Ensign*, Nov. 2007, 18–21.
5. Emily Coburn, "A Sweet Assurance of Life," shared at the Boise, Idaho, *Time Out for Women* on September 14, 2009.

3 Meetings Are Not Rest Stops

Understanding the Many Meetings of the Church

> *"When the outcome of a meeting is to have another meeting, it has been a lousy meeting."*
> ***Herbert Hoover***

I learned about the importance of meetings the first time I received a calling as an adult. I had served in some class presidencies in the Young Women program, but it wasn't until I was called as a Primary secretary in our little branch that I was given a glimpse at how important meetings are for the organization of the Church and how essential they are in allowing us to magnify our callings. We didn't have a lot of kids in our Primary—about twenty, if I remember correctly—but with assignments to give, attendance to keep, teachers to assist, notices to send home, and invitations to activities to prepare, without our presidency's monthly planning meeting and the branch council meeting, I doubt I'd have been able to stay on top of it. But, I must confess, it sometimes felt like I was spending my life in meetings.

As a new member in The Church of Jesus Christ of Latter-day Saints, you're going to find that there are a lot of meetings to attend. Even some of us seasoned members can get overwhelmed sometimes by the amount of meetings it takes to accomplish the Lord's tasks. The Doctrine and Covenants says, "Behold, mine house is a house of order, saith the Lord God, and not a house of confusion" (D&C 132:8). Getting that house in order can be a daunting task, and as a result it takes us imperfect mortals a lot of meetings to get some order. Think about your family and your house and the hard work and trials it takes you to get everyone where they need to be, when they need to be there, with the stuff they need to be there with; and then try to imagine if your family were made up of millions of people and they lived all over the world! Could you still do it without a lot of meetings? I know I couldn't, so I don't expect the leadership of the Church to get us back to our Father in Heaven with all the stuff we need to bring with us without a meeting or two.

More important than the organizational needs of the Church, meetings are to lift us and help our testimonies grow as we study and share our experiences with other members. The Lord knows how difficult it can be with the world churning all around us to find time to share the gospel and learn from other members. He has given us the commandment to meet together as Saints often. Elder F. Melvin Hammond said, "On Sunday we attend our meetings, including sacrament meeting, and during the week we attend any other meetings to which we are invited. We attend to learn more about the Savior, to renew the covenants we made with Him at our baptism by partaking of the sacrament, and to discuss and learn the important truths of the gospel. We are also given an opportunity to mingle socially with our brothers and sisters in this new family and to cultivate eternal friendships."[1]

Without a doubt you'll enjoy some meetings and come away enlightened and with your spirit lifted, but other meetings you'll have to endure. Keep in mind during those arduous meetings that perhaps there is someone else there who will be blessed by the words spoken—just this time it's not you. In order to get the most out of the meetings you attend, follow these four simple rules:

1. Be on Time

Louis XVIII of France is quoted as having said, "Punctuality is the politeness of kings."[2] Not only is it a sign of good manners, being on time is also a huge help in arriving at your meeting in the right frame of mind. I don't mean that you need to be at the meeting hours before it is set to begin, but you should be seated at least five minutes before the meeting is scheduled to start. This will allow you a few minutes to gather your thoughts, enjoy the prelude music, and prepare to be touched by the Spirit.

I grew up in a home of perpetual lateness. We were late for everything—I even think we were a few minutes late getting to the temple on the day we were sealed as a family. Not something to be proud of, I know, but it's the truth. With eight kids to get ready (including seven girls' hair to do), I'm sure it seemed impossible for my poor mom to get up early enough to make sure we were at our meetings on time. It wasn't just Church meetings we were late for. We almost missed the bus more times than I can remember. If our branch president hadn't been our bus driver, I'm sure the memories would be different. Being late drove me crazy. I hated walking into a classroom or, even worse, into the chapel after everyone was already there and ready. I hated having everyone turn to see who was making the noise climbing over chairs, trying to get eight kids sitting on chairs and not each other! It's not that my mom didn't plan to be on time, she just always thought that she had the time to do one more thing on her endless list of things to do before we left for Church, but she really didn't. Sometimes I think we were so rushed and harried from being late that we wouldn't have been able to feel the promptings of the Spirit if they'd been delivered by a two-hundred-fifty-pound football linebacker. What missed opportunities.

Being late throughout my childhood actually turned out to be an amazing blessing for me because, as an adult, I can't stand being late. It bothers me more than almost anything. When I left home to start college at Rick's College (now BYU–Idaho), I vowed that I'd never be late again. I'll admit I didn't make it easy on myself. As a new freshman with the freedom to set up my own class schedule, I had a class that started at eight o'clock every morning. There were many Monday mornings, and a lot of other mornings as well, when the only thing that could compel me to get out of bed and off to class was the vow I'd made to myself to be on time. And surprisingly, that managed to do the trick.

I have continued some twenty years later to be committed to that vow, and with the exception of a sick child, one flat tire, and a blizzard, I can't remember another time when I've been late to a meeting, class, activity, or event. I'll admit that there have been Sunday mornings that, with four little kids, being on time has been a real struggle. But with careful planning the night before and some lightning speed in the morning, it is possible. I've actually gotten so used to being on time that if my family isn't sitting in the chapel ten minutes before the meeting starts, I feel like we're late. I realize that most people probably won't become as obsessed with being early as I have, but I can tell you from experience that you get more out of your meetings if you arrive on time.

2. Be Prepared

Kind of sounds like the Boy Scout motto, doesn't it? It's great advice. If you don't have what you need at the meeting, you won't get what you need from the meeting. If you think you might need your scriptures, take them with you. If you think you may need some books or snacks to entertain and quiet your little ones, by all means, take them too.

Please be cautious of what you bring to your meetings. Many times we young moms forget that our little one's favorite treat can make a horrible mess if ground into the carpet in the chapel or that the toy we think is pretty quiet sounds like a foghorn going off when placed in a quiet chapel during the administering of the sacrament. Don't worry, it's happened to all of us. Just remind yourself next time that a talking toy might be a bit disruptive for church.

Not only do you need things to help you be prepared, you might also need assistance from a person. Do you need help preparing your Primary lesson? Find someone with a bit of experience and ask him for help. If you think you may need some help with your children, ask a friend in the ward to assist you. Many of us have been where you are and are more than willing to help ease your burden.

I'm the lucky mom of four boys ranging from nine to sixteen years old, so for nine years I had a baby or toddler on my lap throughout my church meetings. Before my husband joined the Church, prior to the birth of our third son, it was just me with two little guys under three years of age trying to win the battle each Sunday. At times I wondered why I even bothered to get up early on Sunday morning, bathe and dress the baby and his older brother, and then drive the seventeen miles to church, only to spend my time changing dirty diapers in the bathroom, nursing a baby in the mothers' room, and trying to remind my toddler to be reverent. For several years I felt like I wasn't even hearing what was being said from the pulpit, never mind being spiritually fed. It was exhausting and exasperating all in one. It wasn't until I allowed my visiting teachers to start tending the baby or minding the older brother that I finally felt like I had gotten something from Church. By being prepared for the meetings, I gained a testimony that no matter how much I heard with my ears, just being at Church each Sunday, renewing my covenants with my Heavenly Father as I partook of the sacrament, was a blessing that I needed to get through each week.

3. Be Responsive

There may be times you feel like the message or information given at the meeting does not apply to you or your situation, but life's kind of funny, and it changes. Something you heard at a sacrament meeting months ago may be just the words of encouragement you need to get through a trial today.

Bishop Robert L. Simpson advised:

> Each member of the Church has an obligation to come to sacrament meeting with a desire to learn gospel principles and to be lifted spiritually as he recommits himself through partaking of the sacrament. A critical eye and attitude can usually be satisfied by looking for mistakes or human failings. On the other hand, one who comes with a desire to help his fellowmen and follow the admonitions of the Savior as he renews his covenants can usually find good in every word that is spoken and every note that is sung. The sacrament meeting should be an uplifting experience for all. You may need to be more understanding, more receptive, more loving, and more submissive as you assemble each week with the Saints to be edified by the gifts of the Spirit.[3]

Do you have teenagers? If you do, you probably have a small glimpse into how frustrated our Heavenly Father must get with his unresponsive children. I always thought that I was a fairly intelligent person. I have never failed a test in my life, and except for a brief period of math issues in the third grade, I've always gotten good grades and been on the honor roll. It wasn't until I had a teenage son—now two of them—that I realized I'm an idiot. I still don't think that's true, but there are times when I try to give my boys advice, and they look at me and roll their eyes like I've just said the most ridiculous thing. I must admit, it's disconcerting, not to mention quite annoying.

I'm quite sure that is how our Heavenly Father feels when we roll our eyes at something said in sacrament meeting or when we listen to general conference talks and then decide, "That message wasn't for me, it was for the members who are (older, younger, married, single, and so on)." Just as I almost always know what is best for my boys, Heavenly Father always knows what's best for us and is trying to tell us, if we'd just open our ears, turn off our pride, and listen.

4. Be Reverent

The Primary song "Reverence Is Love" says, "Rev'rence is more than just quietly sitting. . . . I'm reverent, for rev'rence is love."[4] While reverence is indeed more than sitting quietly, that is a great way to start practicing reverence, especially when you have little children. I can remember how busy my oldest son Kade was as a two- and three-year-old. He was never one to sit in front of the TV for hours—fifteen minutes was about all he could stand before he needed to be up and running. But when it came to Sunday and sacrament meeting, he seemed to take on a whole new personality. While I could tell that it was difficult for him to sit still and be quiet, he knew how important it was to be reverent, and he tried as hard as his little patience would let him. I must confess, however, that on one occasion his wiggles and curiosity did get the better of him. I can tell you that the ringing of a fire alarm in sacrament meeting does not do much for reverence in the chapel. Never again did we sit by the alarm!

As an adult member, it's important that we set the example for our little children and even our youth on how to show respect and reverence during our meetings. Do we forget to shut off our cell phones so they ring in the middle of the sacrament prayers? Do we spend our time whispering to someone, sleeping, reading our lesson that we should have prepared already, or, even worse, texting on our phones? How we conduct ourselves in our meetings says more about how we view reverence than any words, threats, or bribes we can offer our children. Our examples can say to our children that Church meetings aren't important and that if you feel like you have better things to do, go ahead and do them. Is that the message we want our children to get? Is that the example we want our youth to follow? On the other hand, if we practice reverence in our meetings, it says to our children that Church is important and that we recognize the sacred nature of the covenants we renew and the messages presented. Which message do you want to send?

The Church as a whole is a friendly, fun-loving group, and often this attitude and atmosphere continue into meetings where they need not be. There are many Sundays in our little branch when it is impossible to hear the prelude music being played in the chapel because of all the visiting going on within the chapel walls. There is nothing wrong with visiting with fellow members—that's how friendships are made. There is, however, a time and a place for that, and in the chapel just prior to the beginning of a meeting is neither the time nor the place.

Learning and practicing reverence in our meetings is not just for new converts and children. As seasoned members, we can all use a little reminder every now and then. Most Sundays in my little branch, the music is playing, and one of our seasoned brethren is busy making the rounds—shaking hands and greeting members of the branch and visitors alike. He gets so wrapped up in his visiting and socializing that he doesn't even realize when the prelude music has stopped or a member of the presidency is standing at the pulpit, waiting to begin the meeting. This kindhearted brother means no disrespect, I'm sure; he's just gotten away from the habit of practicing reverence by "quietly sitting."[5]

The leadership of the Church has recognized that there is a growing issue with the lack of reverence in our meetings and in our buildings. Elder Boyd K. Packer counseled:

> The world grows increasingly noisy. Clothing and grooming and conduct are looser and sloppier and more disheveled . . . Irreverence suits the purposes of the adversary by obstructing the delicate channels of revelation in both mind and spirit. . . . Our meetinghouses are designed so that we may enjoy socials, dancing, drama, even sports. All of these are important. But these auxiliary activities should be subdued when compared with what the world is doing. Music, dress, and conduct associated with them are quite different from what is appropriate in the chapel or classroom on the Sabbath day.
>
> When we return for Sunday meetings, the music, dress, and conduct should be appropriate for worship. Foyers are built into our chapels to allow for the greeting and chatter that are typical of people who love one another. However, when we step into the chapel, we *must!*—each of us *must*—watch ourselves lest we be guilty of intruding when someone is struggling to feel delicate spiritual communications.[6]

As a new convert, the first meetings you'll probably be introduced to are those held on Sunday. These include sacrament meeting, Sunday School, and Relief Society for the sisters or Priesthood for the brethren. We also hold many other meetings during the week and at various times throughout the year that you may not be aware of, understand the reason for, or know the protocol for. You may not know how these meetings are organized and conducted. Let's break it down into three groups: Sunday meetings, meetings held during the week, and special meetings.

Sunday Meetings

Elder Dallin H. Oaks said, "The ordinance of the sacrament makes the sacrament meeting the most sacred and important meeting in the Church. It is the only Sabbath meeting the entire family can attend together. Its content in addition to the sacrament should always be planned and presented to focus our attention on the Atonement and teachings of the Lord Jesus Christ."[7]

Elder Bruce R. McConkie taught, "The Church directs the holding of weekly sacrament meetings in all its organized units. These are the most solemn and sacred meetings in the Church. Their purpose is to enable the saints to renew their covenants by partaking of the sacrament; to receive instruction in the doctrines of the kingdom; to worship the Almighty in song, prayer, and sermon."[8]

The time your Sunday meetings start and the order in which they occur may vary depending on where you live, how many other units (wards or branches) use the same building, and the decision of your local leaders. When we lived in Idaho, we had the opportunity (and I use that word loosely) to experience Church starting at various times. One year we started at 8:00 a.m. That was a rough year, and I'm pretty sure it was at least eighteen months long. The next year we rolled to 12:00 p.m., and I have to be honest—I think I liked 8:00 a.m. better. Our last full year in Idaho, we finally got what one of my friends refers to as the celestial hour: 10:00 a.m. For me, that was the absolute best time to start Church! But different times work better for different people, and regardless of when your meetings start, the teachings are the same.

You'll attend sacrament meeting as a family, but for Sunday School, you'll split up for classes according to your age group. Don't worry, if you're eighteen years old or older, no one is going to ask your age in order to determine which class you should go to, so sisters, you won't have to lie in church. During one of the blocks of instruction time, the adult members will attend either Relief Society or Priesthood, the children will attend Primary, and the youth will attend either the Young Women or the Young Men program. The entire block of Sunday meetings, including sacrament meeting, will last around three hours. No, that's not a typing mistake—the meetings are for three hours, and you'll be expected to attend this block of meetings each and every Sunday, with the exception of those weeks when there are special meetings, which we'll cover later. I know that may sound like a lot of your time, especially if you've come from a lifestyle where you seldom went to church or where you only felt obligated to attend at Christmas and Easter, but it's really not that much when you put it into perspective.

In order to get a bit of perspective, let's take a look at the average American's week. You've got 168 hours in your week—everyone gets the same amount of time. As much as I could sometimes use an extra hour in my day, I've yet to figure out how to make that happen, so I have to work with what we've all got. On average you'll probably spend around 52 hours sleeping—that will definitely be more if you're a teenage boy. That's not some scientific discovery, it's just my observation of the weekend sleeping habits of my sixteen-year-old son. I'm confident that number would be a lot higher if we weren't jumping on his bed, banging on his door, and threatening to dump water on him to get him up before it's time to go to bed again!

Each week, the average American spends 35 hours watching television,[9] 13 hours on the Internet,[10] and 7.6 hours eating.[11] Add to that about 40 hours each week working or going to school, not including your commute, which averages 3.83 hours a week.[12] When you look at it that way, 3 little hours spent showing our devotion and obedience to our Heavenly Father, who gives us blessings beyond measure, really doesn't look like such a big deal.

Meetings Held during the Week

Several meetings are held during the week, but they do not happen every week. The meetings or activities can vary depending on the age and sex of the members. There will be meetings for sisters only, some for couples only, some for children, others for youth, many for youth and their parents, some for the brethren, and some for the entire family to attend together. No matter what kind of meeting or activity you have the opportunity to attend, I encourage you to get to as many as you have time to attend without sacrificing all your family time to do it. I don't recall ever coming home from a Church meeting and thinking that I had wasted my time. More often I come home inspired and replenished by the spirit of the gospel and the fellowship that are ever present in the Church.

For the Women

First, let's discuss the meetings for the sisters of the Church. One such meeting is the Relief Society meeting. Until October 2009 these were called Enrichment meetings, and in some areas they may continue to be called this until we become accustomed to the new name. Relief

Society General President Julie B. Beck spoke at the General Relief Society Meeting and said:

> In counsel with the First Presidency and the Quorum of the Twelve Apostles, it was determined that rather than give these additional Relief Society meetings a new title, all such meetings and activities will now be referred to simply as Relief Society meetings. Individual Relief Society meetings that are held during the week can be called whatever they are: Relief Society service, classes, projects, conferences, or workshops.
>
> These additional meetings can be valuable supplements to Sunday instruction, especially for sisters who serve in Primary or Young Women or who are unable to attend Sunday meetings. These meetings also provide a wonderful place to bring our friends of other faiths and to include Relief Society sisters who do not actively participate in the Church. All Relief Society members and their friends are invited and welcome. However, sisters should not be made to feel that attendance at these meetings is mandatory.[13]

This meeting is usually held once a month and is an opportunity for the adult sisters of the Church to meet together to "teach the skills and responsibilities of womanhood and motherhood in the Lord's plan. It is here that women learn and apply principles of provident living and spiritual and temporal self-reliance, and they also increase in sisterhood and unity as they teach one another and serve together."[14]

What a wonderful blessing these meetings can be in our lives as we fellowship our sisters in the gospel, many of whom we may not have been acquainted with had it not been for our common bond in the Church. It was through these additional Relief Society meetings that I learned some amazing skills and became friends with some amazing women. I remember one Relief Society service meeting in particular.

It was during the Kosovo Conflict of 1998–99 when almost one million Albanian men, women, and children were being displaced from their homes by the civil unrest in the Yugoslavian province of Serbia. The news reports each evening were horrifying to see, as babies were shivering in the cold and mothers tried to tend their little ones in the rain, snow, and mud of the refugee camps that were quickly established by the United Nations in neighboring countries. Those of us in our little branch in British Columbia, Canada, were warm and dry in our homes. We had food and clean water, and our babies were safe, and we wanted to do something to help these sisters of ours on the other side of the world. One sister in our branch made us aware of the Quilts for Kosovo relief project, and our Relief Society presidency quickly thrust us into action. We would tie quilts to send to our Albanian sisters in their time of need. We held a quilting marathon for two days, in which our little branch of twenty-five sisters handmade over fifty quilts to send to Church headquarters in Salt Lake to be added to the thousands of quilts from sisters throughout the world.

It was an amazing experience. As a young mother with two small boys, I had been afraid that it would be difficult for me to participate. With my oldest in kindergarten, I took my two-year-old to the church to see if there was anything that I could do while tending my toddler, Zayne. The other sisters in our branch were so excited to have a fresh set of fingers to tie that Zayne became an excuse to take a break. Every sister who was there took a turn tending my baby so I could offer some service to others. When fingers became stiff and backs became sore, someone would say, "It's my turn to watch the baby!" and we'd all switch places with a laugh and a stretch. I was the youngest sister there, but for those two days there didn't seem to be an age difference. Whether we were in our twenties or in our eighties, we were all sisters working toward a common cause. There was a spirit of love and friendship in the cultural hall of our little church that could not be denied—love among those of us tying those quilts, and a greater love for those who would receive them, people we would never meet. More than ten years later, even though I've moved, those sisters I spent those two days with are still some of my greatest friends, and memories of that experience continue to be a motivating influence for service in my life.

For the Men

Not only are there meetings for the sisters during the week, there are also several meetings or activities that the brethren may attend. There are leadership meetings, if you are called to be part of an auxiliary presidency, the branch presidency, or the bishopric. You may be asked to come to the church during the week for a personal priesthood interview with your home teaching supervisor or a member of the presidency. There may be times when there is a service project for the priesthood to do during the week. The opportunities are numerous, and I encourage you to take advantage of every one that you can attend. I also encourage the sisters to find out about these meetings so you can offer a kind reminder to the priesthood holders in your home. I know that my husband has a great memory; it's just short-term. There are many meetings he would have missed had I not known when they were and been able to offer encouragement to attend.

When I think of weekly meetings for the brethren, the first thing that always comes to mind is church basketball. If you live in an area where you are lucky enough to have a gym in your building or to have access to a gym, someone will inevitably decide that it's time for the guys to play some basketball. I have never been a player in this event, but I have had the opportunity on several occasions to be a spectator, and it can be quite the experience. If you ask a seasoned member about Church basketball, I'm sure you'll get a few snickers and giggles before they tell you that it's great. There's a joke that Church ball is the brawl that begins with prayer, so go forward cautiously into this activity. I'm sure with the right group of guys and the right attitudes, Church ball can be a great way to interact with the brethren in the Church and develop some lasting friendships, so I'll encourage you to go with an eager and forgiving attitude and just leave it at that.

No matter what the activity or meeting is, the priesthood holders in your home should be encouraged to attend and be supported in their desire to attend. Your entire family will be blessed as your sons, husband, and father grow in their knowledge of the gospel and as their testimonies increase through fellowship with others in the Church.

For the Children

There are also meetings during the week for the children in the Primary. For some of these activities, all the children are invited to attend; for others, only those who are a certain age will attend. Probably the most frequent weekly meeting will be for the children aged eight to twelve. These are known as Primary activity days. There are a couple of different kinds of activity days depending on the size and location of your unit. In most areas, the boys will be encouraged to join a Boy Scout troop if there is one that is under the direction of the Church in the area. If there is no scout troop, these boys will attend what is known as the Faith in God program. In the Faith in God program, the Primary boys and girls will meet together, usually twice each month (it may be more or less frequently, as decided by your Primary presidency).

During these meetings, they will work on projects and goals that are found in the Faith in God pamphlets, which your son or daughter should receive from the Primary presidency shortly after his or her baptism. There is a pamphlet designed for the boys and a separate one for the girls, although many of the projects are the same. The one for the boys focuses on a few projects that are Boy Scout related. If there is a scouting program, the girls in those areas will attend a separate meeting that accomplishes the same objectives as the Faith in God program but may be referred to as Achievement Days. The best way to find out what meeting your child will be attending is to check with a member of the Primary presidency. Don't assume that they'll call you individually or make sure you know about it. As a past Primary secretary, I can tell you that most often Primaries give the kids notices, but as a mom I can also tell you that these reminders and notices rarely make it home from church.

Another meeting that will be held for the children is the Primary quarterly activity. Just as the name suggests, these activities are usually held four times a year, and each is an opportunity for the entire Primary, with the exception of the nursery, to meet together to socialize and learn of Jesus Christ and his gospel.

Elder M. Russell Ballard said, "Quarterly activities can be stimulating and fun, but they don't mean much if the children are not there or if they come away having been entertained but not really enlightened, taught the gospel, or lifted spiritually. Teachers need to make sure that they are *not* simply preparing to teach a *lesson*, but rather they are preparing to *teach a child of God*. Every lesson, every meeting, and every activity should be focused on bringing these little ones to Christ."[15]

When I was called to be the Primary president of the branch in Eureka, Montana, it became my goal to make sure our quarterly activities were ones that each child would eagerly anticipate and willingly attend. That was no small task, and I can sympathize with anyone who has this calling. It can be quite daunting. It's not easy coming up with activities that teach a lesson about our Savior that can be appreciated by both three-year-olds and eleven-year-olds. With careful planning and inspired counselors, our Primary had several activities that were enjoyed by leaders and children alike. My favorite by far was our Christmas trip around the world.

During 2008, those of us in the Primary presidency introduced the children to one of the Church's temples at the beginning of each month. We would share a small story about that temple as well as some little-known facts or interesting information that the children might find unique and memorable. We would post a photo of the temple on the wall and connect it with string and a pin to its proper location on our map of the world. Each week of the month we would ask the Primary what we had learned and add a bit more to it. We worked on it all year, and by December our Primary had been introduced to temples from all over the world.

For our quarterly activity we decided that it would be fun for the kids to be able to personalize what they had learned as they came to realize that the children in far away countries were also beloved children of God. We decorated our multipurpose room like the inside of an airplane, provided each child with a boarding pass and a seat assignment for CTR Airlines, and embarked on a Christmas journey around the world. We decorated several classrooms to represent the various countries where the temples were located and hung a picture of the respective temple in each room. As we "landed" our plane, the children were ushered to their country based on seat assignment. While they were in that country, they were invited to sample a treat, learn a Christmas tradition from that country, and make a Christmas ornament to take home. When the afternoon ended, each child and every adult in the room had a smile on his face. Take your children to the quarterly activities. They'll be blessed, and you'll be blessed, even if it's only by getting them out of your hair for a couple of hours.

For the Youth

The young people in the Church will also have meetings held during the week. The most frequent will be seminary. Depending on your location, numbers, and ward boundaries, seminary can take on several different forms.

In a question and answer article in the *Ensign*, Elder Paul V. Johnson, who is responsible for overseeing the seminary program, stated:

> **What's the difference between released-time and early-morning seminary, and what is home-study seminary?**
>
> Seminary is supposed to be a daily experience for everyone. Released-time seminary takes place in areas where schools allow students to be released from school for one class period to attend seminary, which is held off-campus at a nearby Church-owned building.

Early-morning seminary is held before school, sometimes in a chapel and sometimes in a home. Home study is used where members are really spread out and it's not possible to get together every day. Home-study curriculum is designed so that every day you study the scriptures, answer questions, and do activities. Then once a week you get together as a class.

So there's really no place in the world where you can't participate in seminary?

That's correct. In fact, right now we're actually studying the possibility of an online seminary for people who are really isolated. We have seminary students in almost 140 countries right now.[16]

The time spent in seminary will be a wonderful blessing to your child as he learns gospel stories and principles and becomes friends with other youth in the Church. I'm happy to say I'm a seminary graduate. It was not an easy task: I attended home study seminary, and I'll admit there were many times when I was tired of having to do the assignments. I'm thankful for wonderful seminary teachers who worked so hard with me to make sure I completed each course. I'm sure it wasn't easy for them either! I am particularly grateful for Brother Woods, the area seminary coordinator, and for how hard he pushed us to memorize the scripture mastery scriptures. I can still remember the year our little branch was able to win the scripture chase contest in our district. I'm not sure if Brother Woods realized that we had some silly made-up clues that helped us out. I wouldn't say we cheated, but we came pretty close! Sorry, Brother Woods.

Seminary was a trial for me, but I'm equally sure that my attendance in seminary was a trial for my poor mom. In the four years I attended seminary, I know my mom spent as much time sitting at the kitchen table looking up scriptures as I did. Thanks, Mom. Not only did my mom contribute time to my seminary success, but my dad always made sure we had a ride or a vehicle to drive to seminary. Since our family had at least one child in seminary over a nineteen-year period and it was thirty miles round-trip to attend, my parents literally spent thousands of dollars helping all of us attend seminary!

As a parent of an early morning seminary student, I know what a sacrifice it can be to get your child there. Every morning when my alarm goes off, I wish we didn't have to give up that extra hour of sleep, and although the distance to the Church from our house is less than what I drove as a seminary student, it still requires a financial commitment to the program. I know that the knowledge and testimony that my sons are building are worth countless hours of lost sleep and the dollars spent on gas to get them there. Make sure your children attend seminary—it sets a strong foundation for them to build their testimonies on. There may come a time in their lives when that foundation will stand when everything else around them seems to have crumbled. Get them there!

Another meeting for the youth that occurs during the week is Mutual, or the Young Men and Young Women program. These weekly meetings are a time for our youth to socialize together and fellowship one another as they participate in lessons, activities, and service on a more relaxed and fun level than Sunday services. The *Guidebook for Parents and Leaders of Youth* says:

"Young men and young women should have a weekly activity night called Mutual, unless travel or other restrictions preclude it. Well-planned Mutual activities play an important role in the lives of youth. Mutual gives them an opportunity to meet in a social setting, apply gospel principles taught on Sunday, strengthen their testimonies, give service, develop wholesome relationships and communication skills, and reach out to less-active youth."[17]

In a world where LDS youth feel alone and as if they do not fit in, the weekly mutual activities are an opportunity for them to feel as though they have someplace to go for support and others they can turn to as they strive to live the gospel standards. It can be difficult to be the only member in your high school. I was one of only three members that attended my high school, which had a student body of approximately 400 students. One of the other members in the high school was my older sister. We were in each other's face all the time, and since she was a year older than me and had friends of her own, it made it difficult to want to hang out at school. I'll admit, I hated high school. One of the main reasons was that it was so hard to fit in. Not many people in my high school went to any kind of church on a regular basis, and they felt awkward around anyone who didn't curse, wouldn't drink, and had moral standards different than theirs. I don't mean to imply that everyone in my school was a heathen, but as a sixteen- to eighteen-year-old, it was very difficult to be different.

Our Young Women group was made up of girls who lived in a very big area, so there were other girls who went to high school in another town as well as the three of us who attended high school in Fernie, BC. Our weekly mutual meetings were a wonderful opportunity to hang out with friends who had the same standards as we did. Those meetings on Wednesday night were just the boost I needed to get me through the week at school being different. Even as an adult, I still value the opportunity to attend meetings or activities with like-minded, like-valued sisters and receive that little reassurance that different is okay. In fact, in some cases different is great!

In an August 2008 *New Era* article, Christa Skousen wrote:

> In areas where travel to activities involves long distances, where returning home at night might be unsafe, or where Church population is small, local leaders can adapt youth activities to fit their circumstances. In Germany, for example, youth gathered on a Saturday morning for a table tennis (ping pong) tournament. In Tonga, youth cleaned the chapel inside and out and also tidied up the grounds and gardens. And in Ghana, youth gathered in a member's home to sing hymns and talk about worthy music. No matter what country or circumstance the youth were in, they all recognized that by being together they were strengthening each other.[18]

Elder Jeffrey R. Holland reaffirmed the importance of these meetings when he spoke at a worldwide leadership training meeting in June 2004. He said, "I ask you to do everything you can to create or to provide the circumstances for a spiritual experience in the lives of our Aaronic Priesthood young men and the young women of the Church as well. Nothing we do for them in our various programs will matter as much as that, and I promise you it is what they will remember and treasure the most."[19]

Other Meetings

In addition to the meetings previously mentioned, there are other meetings that I have chosen to lump together in one group. Some of these meetings will happen on weekdays, others will be held on Sunday, and some may be held at your regular Sunday meeting time.

Fast & Testimony Meeting

This is the sacrament meeting that is usually held on the first Sunday of each month. "Proper observance of fast Sunday includes going without food or drink for two consecutive meals, attending fast and testimony meeting, and giving a fast offering to help care for those in need. Fasting combined with sincere prayer can strengthen us spiritually, bring us closer to God, and help us prepare ourselves and others to receive God's blessings."[20]

During this meeting, members of the congregation (that's you) will have the opportunity to share their testimonies with those in attendance. There may be times when members will take that opportunity to share a travel log, of sorts, or journal of the many events of their lives. We are counseled to avoid bearing our testimonies in such a way. A testimony "need not be a long, impressive discourse. Your testimony will be most powerful when it is expressed as a brief, heartfelt conviction about the Savior, His teachings and the Restoration."[21]

Elder David A. Bednar taught:

> The bearing of testimony need not be lengthy or eloquent. . . .
>
> We should remember that bearing a heartfelt testimony is only a beginning. We need to bear testimony, we need to mean it, and most importantly we need consistently to live it. We need to both declare and live our testimonies. . . .
>
> A testimony is what we know to be true in our minds and in our hearts by the witness of the Holy Ghost. As we profess truth rather than admonish, exhort, or simply share interesting experiences, we invite the Holy Ghost to confirm the verity of our words. The power of pure testimony (see Alma 4:19) does not come from sophisticated language or effective presentation; rather, it is the result of revelation conveyed by the third member of the Godhead, even the Holy Ghost.[22]

General Conference

Twice each year, members of the Church are blessed by the opportunity to listen to the general leadership of the Church share messages that are specifically pertinent to us in our day. On the first weekend of April and the first weekend of October, general conference is held in the Conference Center in Salt Lake City, Utah. While it is a wonderful experience to attend these meetings in person, the Church also broadcasts the meetings via satellite to the many church buildings around the world. In addition, these meetings may be broadcast on your local networks, depending on where you live. It is also possible to listen to general conference on the radio or Internet, if available in your area.

There are several sessions of conference, and members of the Church are encouraged to view each meeting that is appropriate for them. There are two sessions for the general Church membership on Saturday, followed by a priesthood session Saturday evening for the brethren of the Church. For you sisters who may feel left out, the talks given at this session will be printed in the Church magazines the following month, so you can read the words of our leaders from that evening. It is important that as sisters we encourage our priesthood brethren to attend and not complain that we can't.

I already feel like I have enough to do that I'm not going to worry about what the leadership of the Church wants the priesthood men to do. Just a thought. But don't despair. If you really feel like you need some personal instruction, a general Relief Society meeting is held every fall, and for the young women of the Church there is a general Young Women meeting held in the spring.

Ward and Stake Conferences

In addition to general conference, which benefits the entire population of the Church, you'll also attend your local conferences. Your ward or branch will hold one each year, and the messages heard will be prepared specifically for the needs of your unit. Often your stake presidency will speak, and it is a wonderful opportunity to listen to your area leadership and hear of their love and concern for each of you. Twice each year, your stake will hold a conference. Usually there will be meetings on Saturday for leadership followed by a session in the evening, which is usually designed for the adult membership of the stake and addresses concerns and doctrine for the adults. The Sunday session is for the entire family to attend, and I know it can be difficult to get your little ones to sit still and quietly for two solid hours, but stake conference should never become an excuse not to attend Church.

Training Meetings

General Church leaders periodically hold training for the leadership of the Church. These meetings are broadcast over the Church satellite system throughout the world. They are usually referred to as worldwide leadership training meetings, and they cover a topic of particular interest or need for local leaders. They have focused on such topics as building up a righteous posterity, teaching and learning in the Church, and supporting the family. Additionally, in February 2009 the Church produced a training DVD, *Basic Principles of Welfare and Self-Reliance*, for the use of bishops and Relief Society presidencies worldwide.

Your stake will often hold training or leadership meetings throughout the year in order to assist each person who has been called to a position of leadership to do their calling in the proper order and with the proper spirit. These can be an enormous help when you're looking for ideas or have problems with your calling. You can get some ideas or support from your stake leaders that will help you fulfill your calling to the best of your ability—and that's all anyone, including the Lord, can ask of you.

Socials

Last, perhaps the most fun Church meetings aren't really meetings. They are the ward socials or activities. They provide an opportunity for the members of the ward to get together to socialize and have fun while living the standards of the Church. How many you have, when you have them, and what you do at them will depend on your ward and who the bishopric has called to the activities committee. Attend these whenever you can. They're fun and won't seem like meetings at all!

Elder Adney Y. Komatsu said,

> Activities can be so much more than fun and games, and so much more than momentary pleasure. Activities planned with purpose and carried out with real efforts aimed at helping participants on their path to perfection bring joy everlasting and occupy an important place in the Church.
>
> We need to be reminded that activities sponsored by the Church are not new. . . . Activities have been an important part of the Latter-day Saint way of life. Church activities continue to be one means to include rather than exclude, to be a participant rather than a spectator, to find moments of joy among challenges of adversity, to promote socialization and unity rather than isolation and disharmony, to offer neutral and nonjudgmental circumstances for those who are winning their way back to full fellowship in the Church with the Saints and household of God.[23]

The list of meetings has been long, but so will be the list of blessings you will receive by attending your Church meetings. One of the Church manuals sums up the importance of meetings:

Attending our Church meetings can help us to become more obedient to the Lord's commandments. Church meetings help enlarge our talents, increase our knowledge of gospel doctrines and principles, and develop greater faith and testimony. They strengthen our ties with friends and neighbors who will support us in living righteously. They draw us closer to our Father in Heaven and Jesus our Savior. They help us to have the Lord's Spirit. The Savior has promised that "where two or three are gathered together in my name, there am I in the midst of them" (Matthew 18:20).

Attending Church meetings can help lead us to peace in this life and eternal life in the world to come. Meetings are blessings to us from the Lord.[24]

NOTES

1. F. Melvin Hammond, "New Members, New Traditions," *Ensign*, Oct. 2006, 34–37.
2. "Louis XVIII of France quotes," *ThinkExist.com*, http://thinkexist.com/quotes/louis_xviii_of_france/.
3. Robert L. Simpson, "Q&A: Questions and Answers," *New Era*, May 1971, 32.
4. "Reverence Is Love," *Children's Songbook*, 31.
5. Ibid.
6. Boyd K. Packer, "Reverence Invites Revelation," *Ensign*, Nov. 1991, 21.
7. Dallin H. Oaks, "Sacrament Meeting and the Sacrament," *Ensign*, Nov. 2008, 17–20.
8. Bruce R. McConkie, *Mormon Doctrine*, 2nd ed. (West Valley City, UT: Bookcraft, 1999), 661.
9. Alana Semuels, "Television viewing at all-time high," *Los Angeles Times*, Feb. 24, 2009, http://articles.latimes.com/2009/feb/24/business/fi-tvwatching24.
10. Humphrey Taylor, "Internet Users Now Spending an Average of 13 Hours a Week Online," *The Harris Poll, Harris Interactive*, December 23, 2009, http://www.harrisinteractive.com/vault/HI-Harris-Poll-Time-Spent-Online-2009-12-23.pdf.
11. Karen Hamrick and Kristina J. Shelley, "How Much Time Do Americans Spend Preparing and Eating Food?," *Amber Waves*, Nov. 2005, http://www.ers.usda.gov/AmberWaves/November05/DataFeature/.
12. Joseph Carroll, "Workers' Average Commute Round-Trip Is 46 Minutes in a Typical Day," *Gallup.com*, August 24, 2007. http://www.gallup.com/poll/28504/Workers-Average-Commute-RoundTrip-Minutes-Typical-Day.aspx.

13. Julie B. Beck, "Relief Society: A Sacred Work," *Ensign*, Nov. 2009, 110–14.
14. Ibid.
15. M. Russell Ballard, " 'Great Shall Be the Peace of Thy Children'," *Ensign*, Apr. 1994, 59–61.
16. Paul V. Johnson, "A Higher Education." *New Era*, Apr. 2009, 12–15.
17. "Mutual," *Guidebook for Parents and Leaders of Youth* (Salt Lake City: Intellectual Reserve, 2001), 22.
18. Christa Skousen, "Mutual Benefits," *New Era*, Aug. 2008, 18–23.
19. Jeffrey R. Holland, "Bishops and the Aaronic Priesthood," *Worldwide Leadership Training Meeting*, June 19, 2004, 19, quoted in Christa Skousen, "Mutual Benefits," 18–23.
20. "Fasting & Fast Offerings," *True to the Faith: A Gospel Reference* (Salt Lake City: Intellectual Reserve, 2004), 66–67.
21. "Testimony," *True to the Faith: a Gospel Reference* (Salt Lake City: Intellectual Reserve, 2004), 180.
22. David A. Bednar, "More Diligent and Concerned at Home," *Ensign*, Nov. 2009, 17–20.
23. Adney Y. Komatsu, "Please Hear the Call!," *Ensign*, May 1992, 29.
24. "Church Meetings," *The Latter-day Saint Woman: Basic Manual for Women, Part A* (Salt Lake City: Intellectual Reserve, 2000), 122.

4 Packing for Your Road Trip

A Lesson in What Not to Wear

"Appearances are a glimpse of the unseen."
Anaxagoras

Elder Sterling W. Sill has observed, "A let-down in personal appearance has far more than physical significance, for when ugliness gets its roots into one part of our lives it may soon spread to every other part."[1]

How we dress and how we present ourselves says a lot about the type of people we are. If we dress in sloppy, baggy clothing, it gives others the message that we are sloppy. If we dress in tight, suggestive clothing, it creates in others the impression that we do not value virtue. What does your clothing say about you?

The fashions of the world are continually changing. Unfortunately, they are not changing for the better. Women's shirts are getting tighter and more revealing on both ends. Skirts and shorts are often so tight and short that walking without exposing body parts can be difficult. Even blue jeans, which used to prevent overexposure, are tighter, ride lower, and have rips in areas that prevent them from being modest. Men's clothing, while not exposing skin, is growing tighter, and often exposes others to graphic images, crude and vulgar language, and illegal or inappropriate products. Shopping for clothing can often be a walk on the wild side since most items have been designed to fit the world's standards.

Having just come from the world into The Church of Jesus Christ of Latter-day Saints, many new converts may not realize that the Church has dress and grooming standards. These standards in comparison to the world's are as different as night and day. As members of the Church, we are encouraged and counseled to dress modestly at all times.

Sister Jan Pinborough said, "In many modern societies, standards of modesty and even decency in dress have all but vanished. Styles that once might have been seen only in a cocktail lounge or an inappropriate magazine are now being marketed to children—and at younger and younger ages."[2]

In the pamphlet *For the Strength of Youth*, members of the Church are given guidelines that apply not only to the youth, but to members of every age:

> Immodest clothing includes short shorts and skirts, tight clothing, shirts that do not cover the stomach, and other revealing attire. Young women should wear clothing that covers the shoulder and avoid clothing that is low-cut in the front or the back or revealing in any other manner. Young men should also maintain modesty in their appearance. All should avoid extremes in clothing, appearance, and hairstyle. . . .
>
> . . . If you are not sure what is appropriate, ask your parents or leaders for help.[3]

As a new convert you may not consider your clothing immodest. For many of you, that may be true. "Of course, modesty goes beyond the exact length or style of a clothing item. A crude logo can make even a sweatshirt immodest. Modesty involves both the motives and attitude of the wearer. Those who flaunt their bodies or use them to get attention do not look modest, regardless of what they wear."[4]

At a Women's Conference address at Brigham Young University in April 2004, Elaine S. Dalton, Young Women general president, said:

> Modesty is often talked of in terms of dress and appearance, but modesty encompasses much more than the outward appearance. It is a condition of the heart. It is an outward manifestation of an inner knowledge and commitment.
>
> Modesty is about more than hemlines, necklines, and revealing clothing. It is the appropriate dress for the appropriate setting. It is caring to dress appropriately to show respect for people, places, and settings.
>
> Modesty extends to our actions, our speech, our attitudes, our thoughts, even our desires. Our modesty is a reflection of our desire to follow a prophet of God. I repeat, being modest is more than how

> we dress. Modesty is an outward manifestation of our inward commitment and understanding.
>
> When we are modest, we reflect in our outward actions and appearance that we understand what God expects us to do.[5]

Clearly what we wear says a lot about who we are. Even if your clothing is not immodest, it may not be appropriate. There is a difference. Just as you wouldn't go to the beach in a tuxedo or to a funeral in a swimming suit, there are dress standards that are appropriate for every aspect of your life. The standards can be classified loosely into two categories: casual dress and Sunday dress.

Casual Dress

Elder M. Russell Ballard said, "Be careful how you dress. . . . Dress in such a way that if the Lord came tomorrow and called a meeting together and invited you to attend that you would feel comfortable to be in His presence."[6]

Casual dress is how your appearance is on a regular day of your life when you're not doing anything special or out of the ordinary. For many adult converts this may include the clothes you wear to work or around the house or when running errands. For young converts, casual dress or attire is how you dress to attend school or to go to your job. Regardless of what your everyday activities may entail, casual dress is what you wear.

As with all worldly fashion, the standards for casual dress have changed over the centuries. This change began slowly, but like a snowball rolling downhill, picking up speed and snow on each turn, the damage it can do continues to grow with each passing year. The standards are now less about virtue and appropriateness and more about free expression, shock value, or pushing the limits of what society will tolerate.

I can remember the first summer I had a job. I was twelve years old, and I was a child behavioral enforcement specialist—or as you probably know it—babysitter. (I've learned that a résumé is all in the wording!) With my newfound employment came an abundance of wealth—at least it seemed like that to a twelve-year-old. I saved my wages all summer, which was not an easy task, but I had a plan for my money. After paying my tithing, I was going to buy my own school clothes that year.

My parents always made sure we had one or two new outfits to start school with each fall, but with five kids attending school that year I knew money was going to be tight. I was grateful that year that I had my own money. I'd be able to buy the clothes I wanted and wouldn't have to worry about the cost. It was a great feeling to an independent twelve-year-old.

Waiting for our annual summer trip to my grandma's house was torture, but eventually August came, and with it the long-awaited trip. Gramma lived near what we considered a city but I now realize is just a large town. It's amazing how perspective changes with age. On the day of our school shopping trip, I could hardly sit still on the forty-minute drive to the city. This was before the days of seatbelts and car seats, and with seven of us kids, Mom, and Gramma crammed into the car, my excitement was not well received. When we finally arrived at the mall, I thought I'd died and gone to heaven.

I remember trying on clothes that would have been too expensive had I been using my parents' money. No matter which store we entered, I did not have any difficulty finding clothes that fit the dress standards of our family and the Church. I recall with fondness my favorite outfit from that day: a pair of pale yellow corduroy pants that tapered at the ankle; a grey, yellow, pink, and blue striped long sweater that came about halfway between my waist and my knees; and of course a wonderful pair of grey legwarmers. Oh, weren't the eighties grand? I loved that outfit.

When I returned to school that fall in my new clothes, I did not feel out of place or different from my schoolmates. They were all wearing various combinations of the same outfit—although some hadn't realized that the legwarmers completed the whole look. The world seemed to have some values and morals—and the clothing reflected that.

As the years passed and I began helping my youngest sisters shop for school clothes, the ability to find modest, appropriate clothing in the stores diminished. This decline continues at an alarmingly rapid pace. While I only have boys to shop for (Heavenly Father was wise enough to send only boys to my home), I still experience anxiety and difficulty in the stores as I try to find clothes that reflect the values of the Church and my home. I admire the commitment of my sisters as they struggle to find modest clothes for their daughters. Belly baring shirts and sleeveless tops dominate the clothing racks, and skirts worn by many of the girls in schools today are considerably shorter than the infamous striped sweater of my youth.

As you begin your journey through life as a new member of the Church, you must abandon the styles of the world and carefully consider what your appearance says about what you believe.

Sister Jan Pinborough provides us with some wonderful guidelines to follow when choosing appropriate casual dress. She wrote:

> • If you have been to the temple, wear clothing that completely covers the garment. Even if you have not yet been to the temple, wear clothing that is appropriate to wear once you have.
>
> • Eliminate from your home any entertainment that dulls children's sense of what is appropriate and what isn't. Every visual medium—movies, computer games, television shows, music videos—carries a message about clothing. If a child's favorite pop star dresses provocatively, a young child may want to copy him or her and may begin to think these styles are not so bad.
>
> • If you cannot find appropriate clothing, sew or have someone else sew for your children if possible. . . .
>
> • Even when you or your children are participating in athletics, your clothing can be modest and tasteful as well as appropriate for the activity. If your child is required to wear an immodest uniform or costume for a school or an extracurricular activity, work with the coach, teacher, or principal to find a more appropriate style. You may even need to help your child consider giving up an activity that requires inappropriate dress.
>
> • Don't buy clothing that looks unwholesome or "borderline" simply to help children fit in with or be popular with peers. Help them feel comfortable with looking different by explaining that this kind of "differentness" is one way they can affirm their faith and be a light to others.[7]

I am a big fan of Halloween. I don't know if it is the spooky atmosphere, the costumes, or the knowledge that Christmas is just around the corner, but it's a fun time of the year. The one problem I have with Halloween is the style of the costumes. Each year they seem to get more and more risqué. As a new convert, this time of the year should never be looked at as an opportunity to abandon the dress standards of the Church and take a walk on the wild, forbidden side. Even your Halloween costumes should reflect your respect for yourself and your love for the Savior.

Last Halloween, I had the opportunity to attend a community Spooktacular Carnival. As I sat visiting with a friend who is a faithful member of another Christian church in our community, I was horrified to see two members of our branch enter the building. About the same time I noticed them, my friend Stephanie noticed them as well. She quickly asked me if these two women were not members of our Church. I replied that they were indeed members. She was visibly as shocked as I was. These two sisters who had been members of the Church for more than a year had chosen to dress inappropriately for Halloween. They had body parts spilling out the top and bottom of their costumes, which were complete with fishnet stockings and excessive makeup. They were without a doubt the most scandalously dressed people at the event. The whispers and gasps could be heard repeatedly that evening as those in attendance commented on their choice. Several times that evening, I was forced to explain the principle of agency to nonmembers as I tried to explain that our Church did believe in modest dress and appearance. It was a Halloween I'll never forget—no matter how hard I try! Choose carefully what you wear on every occasion. People are watching and will lose respect for you and the gospel if you do not live your standards.

Sunday Dress

Just as important as appropriate casual dress is appropriate Sunday dress. Elder Jeffrey R. Holland of the Quorum of the Twelve Apostles said:

> We used to speak of "best dress" or "Sunday dress," and maybe we should do so again. In any case, from ancient times to modern we have always been invited to present our best selves inside and out when entering the house of the Lord—and a dedicated LDS chapel is a "house of the Lord." Our clothing or footwear need never be expensive, indeed should *not* be expensive, but neither should it appear that we are on our way to the beach. When we come to worship the God and Father of us all and to partake of the sacrament symbolizing the Atonement of Jesus Christ, we should be as comely and respectful, as dignified and appropriate as we can be. We should be recognizable in appearance as well as in behavior that we truly are disciples of Christ; that in a spirit of worship we are meek and lowly of heart, that we truly desire the Savior's Spirit to be with us always.[8]

Our small branch in northwest Montana experienced what can only be described as a surge of converts. For a period of several months, our branch had at least one baptism each week, and often more. What a blessing it was to the branch and the community as a whole as people heard and accepted the gospel of Jesus Christ.

Unfortunately, the dress standards of our community closely mirror those of the rest of the world. Tiny skirts, sleeveless tops, inappropriate graphics on clothing, and a general sloppy, disrespectful manner of dress are commonplace. From the teachers in the schools to the students in the hallways to the parents in the seats at the baseball games, immodesty is everywhere. By the world's standards there is nothing amiss. As the members of the community became members of the Church, changes began to occur within our little Church branch. Some were for the better, others were not.

Before long, baptized sisters were attending sacrament meetings in sleeveless, low cut, or strapless blouses. Others showed up in sweatpants, jeans, or dress pants. Others chose to wear immodest skirts and even NFL team jerseys. Some of the new priesthood brethren were showing up in dirty jeans, t-shirts, and work boots. Mickey Mouse and Sponge Bob Squarepants frequently attended Primary on the shirts of the new converts' children. Most alarming was the Sunday one of our new members showed up in shorts made from cut off sweat pants, a sleeveless tank top, an ipod, and a Snuggie (a blanket with sleeves).

Because no one had taken the time to teach our converts the standards our Father in Heaven has for his children, our chapel had begun to look no different than the hallways at the high school or the sidelines at the football games. As the appearance of the members began to reflect the standards of the world, a noticeable lack of reverence crept into our chapel and our meetings. Sadly this lack of reverence had a destructive effect on the tender testimonies of many of our new converts, and within a few short months many of these new members became inactive. Dress standards do not have to do with us, they are about something much more important.

Elder D. Todd Christofferson recently addressed this issue:

> It offends God when we come into His house, especially on His holy day, not groomed and dressed in the most careful and modest manner that our circumstances permit. Where a member from the hills of Peru must cross a river to get to church, the Lord surely will

> not be offended by the stain of muddy water on his white shirt. But how can God not be pained at the sight of one who, with all the clothes he needs and more and with easy access to the chapel, nevertheless appears in church in rumpled cargo pants and a T-shirt? . . .
>
> Some say dress and hair don't matter—they say it's what's inside that counts. I believe that it is what's inside a person that truly counts, but that's what worries me. Casual dress at holy places and events is a message about what is inside a person. It may be pride or rebellion or something else, but at a minimum it says, "I don't get it. I don't understand the difference between the sacred and the profane." . . .
>
> . . . It is really not about us. Acting and dressing in a way to honor sacred events and places is about God.[9]

In response to a question sent in to the *New Era* magazine, the following guidelines were given for appropriate Sunday dress:

> Dressing appropriately is less about what our clothing looks like and more about what it means. . . . Women are counseled to wear dresses to promote a certain spirit of reverence. . . .
>
> Similarly, men . . . wear dress shirts, ties, and dress pants. This is to show a spirit of reverence that is not communicated by more casual clothing. . . .
>
> Wearing formal clothing on the Sabbath sets Sunday apart from the rest of the week in our minds and, thus, in our actions. The Lord has given us this counsel regarding our appearance to help us, and those around us, develop a sense of reverence and feel the Spirit.[10]

Dress standards do not only include the clothing you wear; they include every aspect of your appearance. Your hairstyle may not seem like much, but it can be a big deal. President Harold B. Lee said:

> Do not underestimate the important symbolic and actual effect of appearance. Persons who are well groomed and modestly dressed invite the companionship of the Spirit of our Father in Heaven and are able to exercise a wholesome influence upon those around them. Persons who are unkempt and careless about their appearance, or adopt the visual symbols of those who often oppose our ideals, expose themselves and persons around them to influences that are degrading and dissonant. Outward appearance is often a reflection of inward tendencies.[11]

My oldest son, Kade, is a strong-willed child. He has been since the moment of his birth. Since he took his first breath, he's been checking to see where Shan and I have set the line regarding family rules and expectations. We've had a hard-and-fast rule regarding acceptable hairstyles since the day Kade came home from the hospital. In fact, even though he wasn't born with a lot of hair, when Kade was only five days old, it was long enough that it hung over his ears and covered the back of his jammies' collar. Although Shan had not yet joined the Church—that didn't happen for another six years—he was not going to let our son have long hair. While I was taking a brief nap, he loaded my brand new, tiny baby into the car and took him for his first haircut. I woke up and didn't know where they had gone. And I certainly hadn't given Shan permission to get my baby a haircut!

I can look back and laugh at the incident now, but at the time it was almost a marriage-ending blunder. Luckily for him, he was smart enough to have the hairdresser save the little scraps of baby hair in a film canister, and he brought them home to me. The pattern had been set: our sons would have short hair. It was the rule.

Fast-forward fourteen years to the summer before Kade's sophomore year of high school. Kade had decided to grow his hair longer and get a perm. At first it didn't seem like a big deal—he's a good-looking kid, so it was bound to look good. I also considered it a bit of a safe rebellion—it was, after all, only hair. The first little while it wasn't too shaggy or punkish, and the new curls did look good. But, the longer it got, the worse it looked and the worse Kade behaved. He soon became known in our family as "that punk." And as with all self-fulfilling prophecies, if you say it long enough, it will come true. Kade became a punk. He was mean to his little brothers, disrespectful to his parents, and rude to teachers and fellow students. And his room was a complete disgrace!

We couldn't understand what had happened to our Kade. I blamed it on hormones and the pressures from school. I blamed it on TV and the music he was listening to (which I'm sure didn't help the situation). When reading the *Ensign* one day, I came across a quote from President Hinckley that said, "Be clean and neat and orderly. Sloppy dress leads to sloppy manners. I am not so concerned about what you wear as I am that it be neat and clean."[12]

I finally had an answer to our problem. We were at the hairdresser's the next morning. The change in Kade's behavior was as dramatic as the change in his appearance. The punk was gone, and a typical fourteen-year-old was back in his place. Peace returned to our home—or at least as much peace as you can have with four boys. Learn to live the Church standards. It will make all the difference.

Appearance also includes the way we give in to the trends of the world. Look around and you will see that people in the world are tattooed and pierced—often to the extreme. David A. Burton, MD, president of the Salt Lake Eagle Gate Stake, wrote:

> Although tattooing and body piercing have both been around for centuries, they are experiencing an unprecedented surge of popularity today. The fad is no longer limited to "wild" or "rebellious" individuals. . . .
>
> . . . When individuals follow the body-defiling practices of multiple piercing and tattooing, they dull their spiritual sensitivity. Tattooing the body seems analogous to spraying graffiti on one of our beautiful temples. . . .
>
> The greatest antidote to the current spread of body modification is gospel-centered living, which can help us know who we are and what our relationship to God is. Armed with that knowledge, we can respect the sacred nature of our bodies and thus be prepared to resist unwise fads such as tattooing and body piercing.[13]

I'm proud to be a BYU alumna. I'm even prouder to say I am a Ricks College alumna. I always tell people if I could go back and relive any two years of my life, they'd be the two years I lived in Rexburg, Idaho. While I enjoyed the classes I took, the professors who taught me, and my great roommates, my fondest memories come from the many athletic events we attended. During the two years I attended, the Ricks College Viking athletic teams enjoyed a great number of victories. What I remember most about these athletes was not the number of wins they earned or the points they scored, but the way they represented the dress and grooming standards each of us was required to live.

While many of the athletes from the competing schools wore earrings, shaggy, long hair, and tattoos, our Vikings were clean cut and, with the exception of the cultural tattoos worn by the Polynesian athletes, tattoo free. Oh, how I wish that BYU still held their athletes to that high standard. It's such a disappointment to watch Cougar sports and see that the athletes representing BYU—and, in a large part, the Church—look no different than their opponents!

As you strive to live the gospel standards of dress and appearance, you will be blessed. You will realize your worth as a son or daughter of God. Your entire attitude will change. What appears on the outside will be a reflection of your inner commitment to love the Lord and be obedient to his commandments. The message you send will be one of virtue and values for those around you.

Elder D. Todd Christofferson said it best when he said, "You are a Saint of the great latter-day dispensation—look the part."[14]

NOTES

1. Sterling W. Sill, *The Quest for Excellence* (Salt Lake City: Bookcraft, 1967), 38.
2. Jan Pinborough, "Everything Good and Beautiful," *Ensign*, Mar. 2003, 62.
3. "Dress and Appearance," *For the Strength of Youth: Fulfilling Our Duty to God* (Salt Lake City: Intellectual Reserve, 2001), 14–15.
4. Pinborough, "Everything Good and Beautiful," 62.
5. Elaine S. Dalton in a Women's Conference address at Brigham Young University on April 30, 2004.
6. M. Russell Ballard at a fireside in the Salt Lake City Tabernacle on September 19, 1999, to students in university wards.
7. Pinborough, "Everything Good and Beautiful," 62.
8. Jeffrey R. Holland, "To Young Women," *Ensign*, Nov. 2005, 28.
9. D. Todd Christofferson, "A Sense of the Sacred," *New Era*, June 2006, 31.
10. "To the Point," *New Era*, Nov. 2008, 23.
11. Harold B. Lee, *The Teachings of Harold B. Lee*, 219–220.
12. Gordon B. Hinckley, "'I Am Clean'," *Ensign*, May 2007, 60–62.
13. David A. Burton, "I Have a Question," *Ensign*, Feb. 1999, 52–53.
14. Christofferson, "A Sense of the Sacred," 28–31.

5 Life Is Not a Drive-thru

Understanding and Appreciating the Importance of Work

"The only place where success comes before work is in the dictionary."
Donald Kendall

I have four boys who like fast food. I don't know if they like the food itself or if they just like that it is fast. Because of their appreciation for quick and easy without a concern for nutritional facts, we have become quite familiar with drive-thrus. The concept is pretty simple: you make your menu selection, pay the charge for the food, get your food, and drive away. There is no chopping, cooking, or cleaning up to do afterwards—and loading the dishwasher and cleaning up the kitchen can become quite the controversy at our house. The point is that with a drive-thru, you get fed, and you don't have to do much more than reach into your pocket for some cash. I think most of us are aware that while the food we receive isn't gourmet fare and the service isn't five stars, it is easy. The food fills the void, and you didn't have to work to have your needs met. Sometimes that can be nice, but who would want to eat from a drive-thru every meal?

Many of you may be thinking, "Oh, I would love to!" But think about it: bad food made by who knows who day after day. Not only is it bad food, but it's also not really good for you. My husband works away from home fairly often, and his biggest complaint is having to eat out all the time. I know that most of us wives and mothers would gladly switch places with him, but I have to admit, from the few times I have been away from home for an extended period of time, eating out gets old pretty quick. Home cooking with family around is always best!

Unfortunately, much of the world operates on the same principle as a drive-thru: minimum effort for substandard results. And most of the world seems fine with this—just look at the number of drive-thrus in your town. This worldly philosophy has not only become acceptable, but in some instances, it is encouraged. Government assistance programs provide little incentive for recipients to move forward to a state of self-reliance. Many programs reward slothful and immoral behavior by removing benefits if a woman gets married and increasing benefits for having more children out of wedlock. Many schools teach to the lowest levels in the class rather than challenging those students who are at the top. Youth sports programs reward participants just for showing up rather than acknowledging the extra efforts, skills, and dedication extended by those who are determined to succeed.

I have a younger sister who was and still is an amazing volleyball player. As a high school senior, Denise was selected to attend an elite camp and was chosen to represent our province on their traveling team. She is left-handed and almost six feet tall, so she is a wonderful asset to any team. Even though she is in her midthirties, Denise still plays recreationally and is as dangerous as ever as an outside hitter. One day I received a call from her, and she shared an experience she had with her eight-year-old daughter, Trinity.

Trinity is a soccer player, and being athletic like her mom has helped her to become one of the best players in her league. She is, however, only eight years old and has only been playing soccer for three years. She was in her bedroom taking stock of her possessions and came out and excitedly announced to her mom that she had six trophies. Her team does well but has not been the league champion six times in three years—that is impossible! My sister expressed her delight that Trinity enjoyed soccer and that she had received trophies for her efforts. But she did remind her that a trophy given for just showing up really doesn't mean much. Trophies that you earn from hard work mean much more.

When Denise and I discussed the trophies, she expressed how frustrated she has become with teams and leagues that feel like they have to give everyone a reward. By doing this, they have made the awards commonplace and meaningless. Not only that, but they have removed the incentive for athletes to work hard and try to do their best. As we discussed this issue, we realized that while Denise was an amazing athlete and had played several sports for years at a high level of competition, even she had not received six trophies in her athletic career, and here she had an eight-year-old who saw trophies as nothing more than a reward for participation. Where has the value in hard work gone?

As members of The Church of Jesus Christ of Latter-day Saints, we are encouraged to rise above the standards of the world and do and be the best we can.

Elder Jorge F. Zeballos said, "The Lord does not expect that we do what we cannot achieve. The command to become perfect, as He is, encourages us to achieve the best of ourselves, to discover and develop the talents and attributes with which we are blessed by a loving Eternal Father, who invites us to realize our potential as children of God. He knows us; He knows of our capacities and our limitations. The invitation and challenge to become perfect, to achieve eternal life is for all mankind."[1]

It is important to realize that life does not have a drive-thru lane. What you get out of it and what you achieve will be a direct reflection of the efforts, energy, and hard work you put into achieving your goals. This is an eternal principle. You can't get a gourmet meal at a drive-thru, and you can't rise to the top without breaking a sweat. There is no shortcut to success or self-reliance. It takes hard work and lots of it.

President David O. McKay said, "Let us realize that the privilege to work is a gift, that the power to work is a blessing, that love of work is success."[2]

The leaders of the Church, since the restoration of the gospel by the Prophet Joseph Smith, have consistently and continually instructed the members to become self-reliant.

President Joseph F. Smith taught:

> You must continue to bear in mind that the temporal and spiritual are blended. They are not separate. One cannot be carried on without the other, so long as we are here in mortality. . . .
>
> The Latter-day Saints believe not only in the gospel of spiritual salvation, but also in the gospel of temporal salvation. We have to look after the cattle, . . . the gardens and the farms, . . . and other necessary things for the maintenance of ourselves and our families in the earth. . . . We do not feel that it is possible for men to be really good and faithful Christian people unless they can also be

good, faithful, honest and industrious people. Therefore, we preach the gospel of industry, the gospel of economy, the gospel of sobriety.[3]

This counsel is of greater consequence with each economic recession or depression that plagues the earth. President Marion G. Romney counseled the members of the Church during the recession of the 1980s, and since we are experiencing the recession of our times, the counsel is needed once again:

> We face today a whole range of serious economic and social conditions. But facing periods of economic stress, even deprivation, is not new to us as a Church. Historically, the Saints have more than once faced such trials. As a result, the Lord from the early days of the Church has guided his leadership to see clearly certain correct principles. Most Church members of this generation, however, have not personally encountered serious economic and social disruption, and thus from their own experience have not learned how to deal with such problems. The most fundamental principles of temporal salvation include two concepts: providing for oneself—*self reliance*—and providing for one's family—*family reliance*. . . .
>
> . . . No member should desire or seek to voluntarily shift the responsibility for his own maintenance to another. Rather, each member, through work, should seek to find great satisfaction in personal achievement; and thus, he will be entitled to the fruits of his labors—both temporal and spiritual.[4]

Since Old Testament times we have been counseled to work to provide for our needs:

> Go to the ant, thou sluggard; consider her ways, and be wise:
>
> Which having no guide, overseer, or ruler,
>
> Provideth her meat in the summer, and gathereth her food in the harvest. (Proverbs 6:6–8)

Even a little ant knows the importance of work. As the scripture says, they have no ruler to command them, yet they work and gather and store the necessities to meet their needs. Are we not wiser than the ants? We too must develop the ability to provide for our own needs.

An important part of self-reliance is identifying our needs. We must be careful that we do not confuse our wants as needs and then use our resources to try and fulfill those desires. In the society we live in, wanting everything has become second nature to many of us, and our wants have become dangerously blurred together with our needs.

I want a brand new car, but I don't need a brand new car. My 1998 Ford Expedition with over 200,000 miles works just fine to meet my needs. I would like to have a designer purse, but the one I purchased on clearance at Walmart works just fine to meet my needs. It's nice to have a cell phone, but when money is tight it becomes clear that I don't need a cell phone. No one dies if I can't be reached for a while. I enjoy having cable TV, but I don't need to have cable TV. My life doesn't stop just because I don't have it.

I jokingly tell my husband how lucky he is to have me for a wife. Not that I think he's lucky to have married me, but marriage to me could be a whole lot more difficult for him. You see, I'm a pretty practical person. I'll admit that sometimes I lose focus and do confuse my wants as needs, but Shan is always quick to help me get back on track. I'm not sure if that's for my benefit or for his, but it has been a blessing in our family.

Just as Shan helps get me back on track, every member of the family should work together to help the family become self-reliant. In "The Family: A Proclamation to the World," the First Presidency clearly defined the role of each family member. To parents they said, "Parents have a sacred duty to rear their children in love and righteousness, to provide for their physical and spiritual needs, and to teach them to love and serve one another, observe the commandments of God, and be law-abiding citizens wherever they live. Husbands and wives—mothers and fathers—will be held accountable before God for the discharge of these obligations."[5]

To the fathers:

"By divine design, fathers are to preside over their families in love and righteousness and are responsible to provide the necessities of life and protection for their families."[6]

To the mothers:

"Mothers are primarily responsible for the nurture of their children."[7]

I don't want to give the impression that as wives and mothers we should stay at home and, as many joke, eat candy and watch TV while our husbands work to provide for our families. The counsel has been given:

> There is no one perfect way to be a good mother. Each situation

> is unique. Each mother has different challenges, different skills and abilities, and certainly different children. The choice is different and unique for each mother and each family. Many are able to be "full-time moms," at least during the most formative years of their children's lives, and many others would like to be. Some may have to work part- or full-time; some may work at home; some may divide their lives into periods of home and family and work. What matters is that a mother loves her children deeply and, in keeping with the devotion she has for God and her husband, prioritizes them above all else.[8]

Throughout our marriage, at times I have worked outside the home. The first summer Shan and I were married, before our children came, I worked. Shan had an accident and broke his thumb, making it impossible for him to work. Luckily for us, I had been taught to work as a child and had a full-time job that allowed me to fill the void left by Shan's missing paycheck. I worked, and the bills were paid. Mine was not a glamorous, high paying, executive type of job. I had a uniform and fancy job title, Park Facilities Operator, which roughly translated to outhouse cleaner and garbage collector. My point is not to whine about a gross job—and believe me, mine could be gross—but to remember that work is not only an important principle but also an eternal one. All that we are and all that we are able to become will be a result of hard work.

Each word regarding our duties and responsibilities to our families is a verb, and if you remember your grammar lessons from elementary school, you'll realize that verbs are action words. They require us to get off the couch and do something. Long before the Nike Corporation began using the phrase, President Spencer W. Kimball had a plaque on his desk that encouraged members of the Church to "do it!"

Hard times may come upon families due to loss of employment, medical issues, or the death of the financial supporter for the family. Sometimes, despite the best efforts, planning, hard work, and intentions of the family, outside assistance is necessary to meet their obligations. In circumstances such as this, we are counseled to seek assistance first from other family members, then from the Church, and finally from other sources.

> Next to one's own self, the responsibility, the blessing, and great opportunity for lovingly sustaining an individual until he or she leaves mortality rests upon his or her family—parents for their

children, children for their parents. The same covenant that obligates parents to care for their children also obligates children to care for their parents when they need it. . . .

. . . One has no claim on Church resources to resolve personal temporal problems and needs until the family has done all it can to help.[9]

Part of doing all that we can do includes not only developing employable skills or obtaining the education necessary to find employment, but also planning and preparing for the future. According to Elder Robert D. Hales, living a provident life requires effort on our part. He said:

> To provide providently, we must practice the principles of provident living: joyfully living within our means, being content with what we have, avoiding excessive debt, and diligently saving and preparing for rainy-day emergencies. . . .
>
> . . . Our world is fraught with feelings of entitlement. Some of us feel embarrassed, ashamed, less worthwhile if our family does not have everything the neighbors have. As a result, we go into debt to buy things we can't afford—and things we do not really need. Whenever we do this, we become poor temporally and spiritually. We give away some of our precious, priceless agency and put ourselves in self-imposed servitude. Money we could have used to care for ourselves and others must now be used to pay our debts. What remains is often only enough to meet our most basic physical needs.[10]

We have tried to teach our children that the world does not owe you a living, it merely owes you the right to earn a living. You are entitled only to that for which you have worked. This principle has been taught to our boys by lessons, but mostly by example, particularly the example of their father. Shan is a hard worker. I don't know many other people who work as hard to provide for their family as my husband does to provide for ours. Not only is Shan a hard worker, but he's also humble. He has worked jobs other men would probably consider beneath them or just too hard and miserable to be worth the money they provide.

When we were first married, Shan worked logging in the mountains. During the winter this meant he was on snowshoes most of the day, and if you've ever tried to snowshoe, you know it is hard work by itself. In addition to snowshoes, he carried a twenty-five-pound chainsaw, with another five pounds of gas and oil, and his backpack, which contained his saw tools, lunch, water, and hot chocolate in a heavy metal thermos. It was hard work just being there! Once he managed to get to the trees, he had to shovel the snow from around each tree down to an acceptable depth in order to not leave too tall of a stump. With all that finally completed, he then had the dangerous task of felling the tree.

Does this sound like a job for a lazy man? Obviously not. And then consider the weather conditions in which he worked: subzero temperatures, rain, falling snow, wind, sleet—miserable weather of every imaginable form. All this he endured so he could provide for our family. He has since worked as a noxious weed sprayer, sawmill operator, silversmith, hunting guide, general contractor, and handyman. He has taken jobs that paid minimum wage and on some occasions even less. He has worked for people younger than him, with years less knowledge and experience. No matter what, he has worked, and worked hard to support us.

I am grateful for our obedience to the words of the prophets and the desire we have shared throughout our marriage to rely on our hard work rather than the hard work of others to provide for our support. Although it has been difficult on many occasions to pay our monthly bills, we have done it ourselves. What a blessing that has been to us.

As we prepare for the future through living providently, we are prepared to face rainy day emergencies that may come. For some fortunate members of the Church, the storm may never come. For others the rain may be light and quickly pass. For some the tempest may rage long and return often despite your best efforts and earnest prayers. It is during these times that your hard work and your obedience to the teachings of Church leaders will carry you. It will not enable you to avoid the storm completely, but it will enable you to make it through safely.

While we need not be too proud or ashamed to accept assistance when it is our last resort, we must be careful not to fall into a pattern of reliance on others or a habit of idleness. In the Doctrine and Covenants we are told: "Thou shalt not be idle; for he that is idle shall not eat the bread nor wear the garments of the laborer" (D&C 42:42) and that "the idler shall not have place in the Church, except he repent and mend his ways" (D&C 75:29).

When the First Presidency established the Church welfare system in 1936 during the Great Depression, even then they did not view it as a long-term solution to financial problems:

"Our primary purpose was to set up, insofar as it might be possible, a system under which the curse of idleness would be done away with, the evils of a dole [getting something for nothing] abolished, and independence, industry, thrift, and self-respect be once more established amongst our people. The aim of the Church is to help the people to help themselves."[11]

Assistance of any kind, whether it be from family, the Church, or other sources, is intended to be a short-term help to get you back on your feet. It should not be seen as a long-term financial plan. To use it in that way violates gospel standards. President Thomas S. Monson said:

"The assistance given by the bishop is temporary and partial. Remember, Church assistance is designed to help people help themselves. The rehabilitation of members is the responsibility of the individual and the family, aided by the priesthood quorum and Relief Society. We are attempting to develop independence, not dependence. The bishop seeks to build integrity, self-respect, dignity, and soundness of character in each person assisted, leading to complete self-sufficiency."[12]

Not only is Church assistance a short-term program of relief for the necessities of life, it is also to be used only by those who have no other options. Elder L. Tom Perry said:

> The Church welfare system was never designed or intended to care for the healthy member who, as a result of his poor management or lack of preparation, has found himself in difficulty. It was designed to assist the membership in case of a large, physical disaster, such as an earthquake or a flood. It was designed to assist the ill, the injured, the incapacitated, and to rehabilitate them to a productive life.
>
> In far too many cases, members who should be making use of their own preparedness provisions are finding that there is nothing there and that they have to turn to the Church.[13]

In addition to being counseled to work to provide for our needs, we as Church members have also been counseled to work to care for the things we have been blessed with. Regardless of how much money you have or how much you don't have, you can take care of what you have. I have learned that you can be poor without living like you are poor, and the opposite is also true: You can live poor without actually being poor. There is an old expression that says, "fix it up, wear it out, make it do, or do without." Oh, how blessed we would all be if we could learn to make that one of our guiding principles in our families.

I grew up in a great family on a farm in British Columbia. When I was young, our family was probably "poor" by the financial standards of the world, but you would not have known it by the way we lived. Our home was not large, and the entire twenty years my parents lived there, the basement was never finished. There was no drywall on the ceiling, curtains served as doors for closets, and the interior walls that were also part of the foundation were painted cinder blocks. The thing I remember most was that despite the size or quality of our home, it was always clean. I'm confident that with eight kids, this was not an easy task for my mom. Dishes were never left piled in the sink (and we never had a dishwasher). Floors were swept or vacuumed sometimes two or three times a day, depending on how much dirt we tracked in on the bottoms of our shoes or bare feet. The sheets on every bed were changed and washed once a week. Laundry was a constant battle, but dirty clothes were not allowed to sit unattended in piles on bedroom or bathroom floors.

Most impressive, however, was that the outside of the house received as much attention as the inside did. There were always flower beds and baskets that adorned our home, and rather than a dirty, muddy mess outside the front door, we enjoyed a mowed lawn at least two acres in size. It used to drive my dad crazy that he was never allowed to park by the house because of the lawn. The parking spot for the vehicles was almost fifty yards from the house so that there wouldn't be mud outside where we kids wanted to play. As an adult, each time my husband and I have moved, one of the first things I have done is beautify the outside of our new home, even homes we were only renting. When we began construction of our current home, I planted flowers before we had even poured the concrete for the foundation.

From the days of Adam in the Garden of Eden, man has been commanded to care for the home. In Moses the Lord says, "And I, the Lord God, took the man, and put him into the Garden of Eden, to dress it, and to keep it" (Moses 3:15). President Kimball gave us counsel on this several times. In October 1974 he said,

> Now we ask you to clean up your homes. . . .
>
> . . . We urge each of you to dress and keep in a beautiful state the property that is in your hands.[14]

In general conference in the spring of 1976 he again commanded us to clean up our homes. "Whatever your circumstance, let your premises reflect orderliness, beauty, and happiness."[15]

Nothing speaks of more laziness and lack of gratitude for your blessings than a home that is dirty and unkempt. Taking care of your home will create in you a sense of satisfaction and accomplishment that will lead you to a feeling of confidence in your abilities to do other things as well. Do the work. The rewards will come, and they are worth it!

In addition to and more important than taking care of our homes is taking care of our children and families. We are told that our children are our greatest blessings, and as such they should be treated with love, respect, and care. Being a parent is easy. Being a good parent takes hard work and continual effort. President James E. Faust said:

"To be a good father and mother requires that the parents defer many of their own needs and desires in favor of the needs of their children. As a consequence of this sacrifice, conscientious parents develop a nobility of character and learn to put into practice the selfless truths taught by the Savior Himself."[16]

Our children don't need to have clothing in the latest fashions; in fact, it's probably a good idea not to worry about fashion. They don't need to have a closet full of the best and most expensive clothes, but we should work to ensure that they have clothing that is clean, tidy, appropriately sized, and in good repair. They should also be properly dressed and well groomed for what they are doing and where they may be going. I know for moms of boys this can seem to be an impossible and never-ending task, but with effort and a willingness to put your children first, it can be accomplished. I don't mean that your kids should never be allowed to have fun, get dirty, and even wear something totally off the wall—quite the opposite. However, there is, as with everything, a proper time and place for this kind of appearance.

I love puddles! I hate mud, but I love puddles. Who can resist the urge to jump—SPLASH—right into the middle of a puddle? Even as a grown-up I have a difficult time not wanting to give a puddle a good splash now and then. Apparently, this may be some weird genetic disorder—I'm not sure where it's found on the DNA chain, but I know it must be there because every one of my boys *loves* puddles.

As a young mom, this provided some serious stress at times. I thought a "good" mom who cared about her children would never let them play in puddles and get covered with mud. How wrong I was. I quickly learned that a "good" mom joins them every now and then for a splash and lets them stay in the mud all day if they want to. That became the rule in our house: If you want to play in the puddles, go ahead and play! You had one mud outfit per day. You could play in the mud as long as you wanted, but when you came into the house and got cleaned up, the mud was done for the day. Some of my favorite pictures are of my boys when they were little, covered in mud from head to toe. But they never left our home dirty and looking like little street urchins.

Your children don't have to be spotless all the time—that would be impossible. But when you take them to church or send them off to school or the many other places their little legs may go, you need to make sure they go appropriately dressed and groomed. Their clothing doesn't have to be new. My boys have spent most of their lives in hand-me-down clothing or clothing purchased secondhand. It's not new, but it has always been clean, fit them properly, and been mended when needed. Their little bodies have received the same care and attention as their clothing. They are clean, their hair is trimmed, and they've looked as though they are important to someone—because they are! They're my most important somebodies.

Kids can be mean, especially as they get older. They're also very observant. They notice when someone smells funny, when someone's hair is matted and dirty, and when someone's clothing is too small or dirty or ragged. They notice when someone looks unloved. All these things can unfortunately become a starting point of teasing and ridicule. Don't allow your children to suffer because you didn't put in the work to care for them as they deserve.

Doing laundry isn't fun, but in most cases, it really isn't hard work. Running a brush through a child's hair takes only a few seconds but can make an enormous difference in not only how they are seen, but also how they feel about themselves.

There are seven girls in my family. That means there was a lot of brushing that needed to be done before we left the house. My mom is a master with a hairbrush. She could brush our hair and have us all styled in less than five minutes, I'm sure. She had the fastest brush in Canada. My dad still jokes that when Mom would line us all up and brush our hair, she brushed so fast you couldn't see the brush. You could only see the smoke from the friction.

I hated to have my hair brushed. It was fine and tended to become knotted rather easily. I would try everything to get out of having my hair brushed, but I knew that I wouldn't be allowed to leave the house looking like an orphan, so into the line I'd go and endure the brush. Looking back, I realize that it would have been much easier for my mom to let us leave the house without the brushing, but she loved us enough to take the time to make sure we looked loved.

This principle can be applied not only to your children, but to yourself as well. You are a child of God. He loves you. Take the time to be your best. I'll admit I have a day every now and then when I stay in my pajamas all day long. We affectionately call them "jamma days" at our house. They're a rare treat and don't happen very often. Most days we're all up, dressed, and off on our daily pursuits by 8:00 a.m. While the "jamma days" are a nice break, it's difficult to get motivated and get much accomplished if you're wearing your sleeping clothes.

Elder Neal A. Maxwell said:

> I do not believe people can be happy unless they have work to do. One can really be more of a slave to idleness than to work. Work also keeps us humble and reminds us of how all our blessings come to us from our Heavenly Father. . . .
>
> The gospel of work is a very important teaching of the Church. If we learn to work early in life we will be better individuals, better members of families, better neighbors, and better disciples of Jesus Christ, who Himself learned to work as a carpenter.[17]

Get up, get dressed, get going! That's not a lot to do. Even the drive-thru takes a little effort.

NOTES

1. Jorge F. Zeballos, "Attempting the Impossible," *Ensign*, Nov. 2009, 33–34.
2. Quoted by Franklin D. Richards, "The Gospel of Work," *Improvement Era*, Dec. 1969, 101.

3. *Gospel Doctrine* (Salt Lake City: Deseret Book, 1939), 208.
4. Marion G. Romney, "Principles of Temporal Salvation," *Ensign*, Apr. 1981, 3.
5. "The Family: A Proclamation to the World," *Ensign*, Nov. 1995, 102.
6. Ibid.
7. Ibid.
8. M. Russell Ballard, "Daughters of God," *Ensign*, May 2008, 108–10.
9. Romney, "Principles of Temporal Salvation," 3.
10. Robert D. Hales, "Becoming Provident Providers Temporally and Spiritually," *Ensign*, May 2009, 7–10.
11. Marion G. Romney, "Church Welfare Services' Basic Principles," *Ensign*, May 1976, 120.
12. Thomas S. Monson, "Guiding Principles of Personal and Family Welfare," *Ensign*, Sep. 1986, 3.
13. L. Tom Perry, "The Need to Teach Personal and Family Preparedness," *Ensign*, May 1981, 87.
14. Spencer W. Kimball, "God Will Not Be Mocked," *Ensign*, Nov. 1974, 4.
15. Spencer W. Kimball, "Family Preparedness," *Ensign*, May 1976, 124.
16. James E. Faust, "A Thousand Threads of Love," *Ensign*, Oct. 2005, 2–7.
17. Neal A. Maxwell, "Friend to Friend: Gospel of Work," *Friend*, June 1975, 6.

Who Made the Snacks?

Learning to Be of Service

"The vocation of every man and woman is to serve other people."
Leo Tolstoy

The Church of Jesus Christ of Latter-day Saints is unique. I know that probably comes as a shock to you as a new convert—it shocks me every now and then! Perhaps the most unique aspect of the Church is its use of volunteer service. The Church operates with a voluntary, unpaid ministry. That means the presidents, bishops, teachers, and so on for the most part do not attend schools or receive a special certificate or diploma that distinguishes them from the general membership of the Church, nor do they receive pay for the work they do in the Church. (One exception is the individuals who have been hired as seminary teachers in the Church Education System.) Those who serve in the Church are called to serve. Every member of the Church, including you, will have the opportunity to serve at some time or other. This is not a lazy man's church.

Elder Derek A. Cuthbert said, "Service changes people. It refines, purifies, gives a finer perspective, and brings out the best in each of us. It gets us looking outward instead of inward. It prompts us to consider others' needs ahead of our own. Righteous service is the expression of true charity such as the Savior showed."[1]

As a new member, you'll be called upon frequently to be of service. You'll be encouraged to serve in a variety of areas of your life: in your home and family, in the Church, in your community, and in the world as a whole. The biggest and most common opportunity for service will be within the walls of your home. Whether you are married or single, a parent or a grandparent, a sister, a brother, or an only child—you'll have the opportunity to serve.

If you're lucky enough to be a parent, you've undoubtedly had millions of opportunities to serve. From the day you brought your tiny baby home until you leave this earth, you will be serving. Think about the nights you slept little if at all because you just had to make sure your sick child was all right, the hundreds of diapers you changed, the magic kisses applied to "life threatening" wounds, and the nights you've lain awake listening for the sound of the car in the driveway as your teenage driver came home. As we serve in our families, it's important to remember that not every act of service is going to be monumental or life changing. It is the small daily acts of service that have lasting effects.

I have a sixteen-year-old son, which means I sometimes feel as though I have a pig living in my house. He's a great kid, and I love him to death, but he's a slob. Most days the only part of the floor in his room you can see is the small triangle of carpet in front of his bedroom door. He's super busy with sports, seminary, Young Men activities, homework, and family chores, so his room gets neglected. Not only is time a factor in the mess, but I also think it's his little act of rebellion, and since it's not a rebellion with eternal consequences, I cut him a little slack on cleaning every now and then. Eventually, his room does get to the point where I have to intervene.

Even though it's disgusting and takes a while to get it done, about once a month I take the time to clean his room for him. Not only does it make me happy to see the floor in his room, but the feeling I get when he comes home after a late practice and discovers the surprise is worth the effort every time. Even though he's sixteen and quite capable of doing it for himself, the blessings we both receive as a result of my service is always worth the effort. I love it when he peeks his head into my bedroom, gives me his sly grin, and says, "Thanks—love ya, Mom!"

Giving service is important in your family, but equally important is being able to receive service. Allowing others to serve you blesses each person involved. As a parent, particularly as a mom, it may be difficult to allow your family to serve you.

I'm a bit of a control freak—at least that's what my boys say. I have to be the one to push the shopping cart at the grocery store. I have a specific way I like the bath towels folded. I load the dishwasher from the top rack down, and always with the dishes in the same place. Okay, maybe I am a bit of a freak—but it's just the way I like things done. Because of this "flaw" (I hate to use that word), allowing my family to serve me can sometimes (actually, most times) be difficult for me. I know as soon as they begin that the towels will be folded "wrong," dishes will be in the wrong place, and I won't be in control in the store. Many times I've robbed my boys of blessings they would have received if I had been a good recipient of service.

The summer of the tenth anniversary of my twenty-ninth birthday, my wonderful husband made arrangements for me to attend a concert out of town. I was to be away overnight, and my husband and boys would be left home alone. I knew there was a good chance I would return home to find the house in a mess. Rather than forgo the adventure and fun the out-of-town trip would bring so I could stay home and police the laundry and dishes, I released my control and went to the concert.

When I arrived home, my husband and the boys were all still alive, which in and of itself was amazing. To my surprise, they had actually cleaned up after themselves—a huge act of service, since I know how much my guys hate doing laundry and dishes. I've spent way too much time spoiling them all. Of course, the towels were folded "wrong" and the dishes were missing for a couple of days until I was able to find them in a different cabinet. My youngest was thrilled to have folded laundry all by himself, and he could hardly wait to show me how he'd folded and put away my laundry as well. The joy I received from the service rendered to me at home completely overshadowed the fun I'd had at the concert. Learn to accept service from your family—it is so worth it.

In addition to serving and being served, another important element of service in your home should be to teach your children to serve. As you teach your children to serve, remember the greatest teacher is a good example. As your children see you serve and as you involve yourself in service with your children, they will learn the importance of service. The acts of service don't have to be overwhelming, expensive, or extremely time consuming, but they do need to be frequent and meaningful.

My sister Denise shared a personal experience of service with me, which she generously allowed me to share with others. When she gave birth to her third daughter, Presley, one of the sisters in her ward volunteered to bring dinner to the new mom and her family. This sister from the ward purchased a dozen rolls from the bakery and a couple of cans of clam chowder, which she poured into a microwavable container.

While this was something my sister could easily have done herself, it was the intentions of the sister that were important, not what the dinner consisted of. Denise said that this has become somewhat of a standing joke in their home when someone in the ward needs meals brought in—she and her husband say that he'll pick up the rolls if she'll open the soup. Not every meal you deliver has to be homemade.

Teach your children to serve outside the home, but also teach them to serve each other. As you encourage—and sometimes compel—your children to serve, they learn to love each other. Elder Marvin J. Ashton said,

> Day-to-day acts of service, whether for good or evil, may not seem important, but they are building cords of love that become so strong they can seldom be broken. . . .
>
> . . . We serve that which we love. If we sacrifice and give our love for that which our Father in Heaven asks of us, it will help us set our footsteps upon the path of eternal life. Again I conclude, what we serve we learn to love, and what we love takes our time, and what takes our time is what we love.[2]

The family of my youth would be considered enormous by today's standard. I was the second child born in a family of eight children. We lived in a rural area of southern British Columbia, and although both my parents were hard workers, the logging and ranching industries in which my dad worked to provide for our family were unpredictable and often financially unstable. My mom worked in a neighboring town as a registered nurse, which ensured that we always had the necessities of life, if not the luxuries. It wasn't until I was an adult with children of my own that I began to realize how difficult it had been for my parents to provide for our family.

Even though we struggled financially, my parents were then and continue to be wonderful examples of service and charity. We served together as a family as we worked side by side in the huge garden my mom always insisted on planting. I'm confident that my mom is the fastest weed-puller in the world! A lot of what was grown in our garden never made it to our table. It would be delivered to people in our community and extended family who had fallen on hard times and could use some help. No one ever had to ask; my dad always seemed to know who could use a bag of potatoes or a few pounds of meat from one of his steers or pigs that had just been picked up from the butcher shop. Dad always knew who didn't have enough firewood to make it through the next cold snap—and Canada can have a lot of those in a long winter. I can't begin to recall the number of times we went visiting (or as my family calls it, toodling) with Dad and we'd leave something when we left.

These random acts of service and charity happened all year long, but the childhood memories from many Christmases stand out the most in my mind. Not a single Christmas of my childhood passed without Mom or Dad bringing to our family's attention a family in our community who could use some help. Closets and toy boxes were sorted through for things to be given to the family—we were always encouraged to give our best. We'd work with Mom to box up food from our freezers, pantry, and cellar and help her bake the best homemade bread in the world. Dad always made sure there was a Christmas tree, freshly cut from the forest, added to the pile. For us kids the most fun part was always the secret delivery. Not wanting to be caught on our "Secret Santa" missions, we'd always try to devise a way to unload the pile of gifts and get them safely to the door or into the other family's car without one of us kids dropping something or fighting over who was going to knock on the door. What fun we had!

I don't remember a single present I received from all those Christmases (except for the year my older sister found my present and told me what I was getting). But I can remember vividly the many times our Christmas was about someone else. Those were the best Christmases of my youth.

As we served together, we learned the true meaning of love from the wonderful examples of my parents. Their examples have not only blessed my life, but they are now also blessing the lives of my husband and boys as I carry forward the traditions of Christmas service. Every year since we were married, regardless of our own financial circumstances, my husband and I have done a "Secret Santa" project. We've sewn quilts for the homeless—not an easy task with boys—and then delivered them to the people who needed them. We've given copies of the Book of Mormon and Church Christmas movies to nonmember friends. We've left boxes of gifts on the doorsteps of many families and given money to beggars in the cold. As I reflect on our experiences, I realize that we've never missed the money given, we've never regretted the time spent, and as a family we've come away from each experience more united, compassionate, and loving. "Selfless service is an essential ingredient for a full and happy life."[3]

As a new convert to the Church, you will be called upon to be of service in the Church often and in various areas. The variety of callings within the Church is great. At first you may feel that you aren't capable of rendering the service you're called upon to perform. Do not worry. When we feel inadequate, we must follow the counsel of Elder Henry B. Eyring when he taught:

> You are called of God. The Lord knows you. He knows whom He would have serve in every position in His Church. He chose you. . . . The person who was inspired to recommend you for this call didn't do it because they liked you or because they needed someone to do a particular task. They prayed and felt an answer that you were the one to be called.
>
> . . . It was prayer and revelation to those authorized of the Lord which brought you here. Your call is an example of a source of power unique to the Lord's Church. Men and women are called of God by prophecy and by the laying on of hands by those God has authorized.
>
> You are called to represent the Savior. Your voice to testify becomes the same as His voice, your hands to lift the same as His hands. His work is to bless His Father's spirit children with the opportunity to choose eternal life. So, your calling is to bless lives. That will be true even in the most ordinary tasks you are assigned and in moments when you might be doing something not apparently connected to your call. . . .
>
> . . . You see, there are no small callings to represent the Lord. Your call carries grave responsibility. But you need not fear, because with your call come great promises.[4]

The first calling most new converts receive is that of home teacher for the brothers or visiting teacher for the sisters. This calling is a great opportunity for you to develop friendships within the Church. As you visit with and teach the members, your testimony and gospel knowledge will grow. You may also have the opportunity to render service to the families you are called upon to visit. While these opportunities may not always be convenient, do your best to serve when you are able and to do so with a willing spirit. A good friend once told me, "If you complain as you serve, you don't get the blessings. Don't shortchange yourself because of a bad attitude."

Several years ago, my family decided to go skiing on Christmas Eve day. We figured the hill wouldn't be busy as families traveled out of town or parents rushed to get last-minute shopping and errands completed.

We were right—the hill was not busy. Unfortunately, it had been busy the day before, and the soft snow from the previous day had been converted to slick and bumpy ice. Since I had skied plenty of times before, I wasn't too worried about the conditions. My sister Holli and I decided that rather than attacking the hill, we'd just have a leisurely day of laid-back enjoyment. That lasted until just before lunch, when I caught the edge of my ski on a solid chunk of ice and crashed. My skis went one way, and my left knee went the other. I enjoyed a comfortable, although rather scary, ride down the hill in the first aid sled of the ski patrol and later that evening was informed by the emergency room doctor that I had torn my knee to pieces.

At the time I had a one-year-old baby at home and a clothes dryer that had decided not to dry. Within days, my house was a disaster. Unable to drive, I couldn't even haul the laundry up the hill to my mom's laundry room. Mom would stop every evening on her way home from work to pick up a basket of laundry, but with a baby in diapers and a husband who worked felling trees in the forest, we were making much more than one basket of dirty laundry a day. By the end of the week, we had accumulated what I can only describe as a mountain of laundry.

Friday morning, I heard a knock on the door, and as I wheeled myself to the entry with my husband's office chair, I could see my visiting teacher standing on the porch. I was almost too embarrassed to let her into the house, but I thought it would be rude to leave her out in the cold, so I let her in. She took one look around at the disaster zone and immediately got to work. She vacuumed the rugs and swept the floors and then began to haul the mountain out to her van.

Monday morning, she was back at my door with several casseroles that could be frozen for future dinners and the conquered mountain. She had spent her weekend—time she could have spent enjoying her own family—doing my laundry and preparing food for me. Not only was my laundry dry, but it was also neatly folded. Shirts and dresses had been ironed and placed on hangers, and it was all neatly stacked in laundry baskets that she must have borrowed from every sister in our branch. She spent the morning at my house, changing the bed linens, cleaning the bathrooms, and putting away the mountain of clean laundry she had returned to my house. I don't know what blessings she received, but I know my testimony of the importance of visiting teaching and Christlike love was fostered by her selfless act of service.

As I discussed the principle of home and visiting teaching with my husband, he expressed a need within the Church for people to not only do their home and visiting teaching, but also to be home teachable. He said that nothing can be more frustrating or discouraging than being assigned to visit a family who makes it virtually impossible to fulfill your calling. When you set appointments to visit your families and then they aren't home when you arrive, or when they restrict their willingness to have home teachers in their homes to one specific day or hour of the month, it robs others of the opportunity to serve. Be home teachable!

If you gain nothing else from this chapter, I hope you will understand two basic concepts of service:

SERVE WILLINGLY

I was a Primary president for two and a half years, so I know there will be days or even weeks when this will seem to be an almost impossible task, but the Lord is counting on you! He called you! He needs the abilities and talents he gave you to bless the lives of others.

President Spencer W. Kimball said:

> God does notice us, and he watches over us. But it is usually through another person that he meets our needs. Therefore, it is vital that we serve each other in the kingdom. The people of the Church need each other's strength, support, and leadership in a community of believers as an enclave of disciples. . . . So often our acts of service consist of simple encouragement or of giving mundane help with mundane tasks—but what glorious consequences can flow from mundane acts and from small but deliberate deeds.[5]

GRACIOUSLY ACCEPT SERVICE

In some ways it is a lot easier to serve than to accept service. Pride can make it hard for us to receive heartfelt assistance. But refusing to accept service not only denies our friends a chance for growth but may also hurt their feelings.

> When loving service is offered to us in fulfillment of a real need, we can give service to the server by simply accepting the gift and then expressing our sincere gratitude. A simple thank-you is nice. A follow-up card is always welcome.
>
> Sometimes we accept service selfishly without even realizing it. For example, do you realize that your Scoutmaster is rendering

> you a service at great personal sacrifice of time and effort? Have you stopped to think of the service your Sunday School teacher gives? And who serves you more than your parents? Don't forget to say thank you. When service is accepted with the same love with which it is given, it brings joy to everyone.[6]

Seek out opportunities to serve. Serve in your families, serve in the Church, serve in your communities—just serve! The blessings you receive from the service will strengthen your testimony, increase your love for others and for your Savior, and enrich your life eternally.

NOTES

1. Derek A. Cuthbert, "The Spirituality of Service," *Ensign*, May 1990, 12.
2. Marvin J. Ashton, "We Serve That Which We Love," *Ensign*, May 1981, 22.
3. Kenneth Johnson, "We All Have a Father in Whom We Can Trust," *Ensign*, May 1994, 29.
4. Henry B. Eyring, "Rise to Your Call," *Ensign*, Nov. 2002, 75.
5. Spencer W. Kimball, "There Is Purpose in Life," *New Era*, Sep. 1974, 4.
6. "FYI: For Your Information," *New Era*, Mar. 1988, 55–59.

7 Avoiding the Mud and the Potholes

Being in the World but Not of the World

"It's a rough road, there is no denying that. We as drivers need to drive according to the conditions."
Ben Rogers

Everyone comes from somewhere—that's the plain and simple truth of it. Everyone has a place where they have family, friends, neighbors, coworkers, teammates, or acquaintances. When you made the decision to join The Church of Jesus Christ of Latter-day Saints, you made the decision to change your life. President James E. Faust said:

> True conversion changes lives. . . .
>
> . . . If we will turn to the Lord and believe on His name, we can change. He will give us the power to change our lives. . . .
>
> . . . Each new day that dawns can be a new day for us to begin to change. We can change our environment. We can change our lives by substituting new habits for old. We can mold our character and future by purer thoughts and nobler actions.[1]

Unfortunately, most of the people in your life will not arrive at the same place as you at the same time. One day they too may reach the point where they will embrace the gospel of Jesus Christ and join the Church. But for most converts, one of the most difficult trials is accepting the standards of the Church, which may be new and different from the standards of other people in your life—people you have interacted with each day and, in some cases, have a deep, loving relationship with. It would be so much easier if joining the Church meant moving to a place where everyone was a worthy member and was living the gospel standards. It would be easier, but it would not help you to grow and progress. As you struggle to live the gospel standards and stay true to the covenants you made at your baptism, your testimony grows. Without the struggle, you would be denied the experience to see how your life has changed and improved because of your conversion.

Imagine taking a vacation to a foreign country. You are so excited to experience the culture, food, scenery, and language of that country. You plan and pack weeks in advance. The excitement continues to build until finally, after what seems like forever, the day has arrived. You board the plane and begin your adventure. When the plane touches down on the runway in the foreign land, you gather your belongings and begin shuffling toward the door with the other passengers. As you catch your first glimpse of your dream vacation spot, you realize it looks a lot like home. The closer you look, the more similarities you see. Before long you realize the scenery is the same, the smells are the same, the people speak the same language, and even the rain that was falling when you left home has seemed to follow you. If you didn't know better, you'd swear that you had never left home.

Because you're on vacation, you decide to make the best of it and enjoy yourself. For the first little while, the excitement of being on vacation seems to do the trick, and you have fun. After a couple of days of trying to do new things, you realize that everyone around you seems to be having fun doing the same things you did at home. It would be so much easier to just join in rather than read the travel guides and try to find fun and interesting things to do on your own. People around you point you out as a foreigner and make fun of you and the things you're doing. After a short time, you think this vacation isn't as rewarding as you thought it would be, and you become more and more tempted to just join in with the crowd. You decide to pack up and go home and get back to your old life and forget about taking "weird" vacations.

As you've probably realized, this "vacation" is an awful lot like joining the Church. At first you're so excited to be a new member. You make covenants and are prepared to live up to each one of them. By and by you realize that nothing else around you has changed: your old friends are still around and are having fun doing all the things you used to do, the music on the radio is still the same, Hollywood is still producing the same types of movies, the Internet still opens doors to all kinds of evil, and the language you hear every day has remained the same. The only thing that is different is you!

You continue trying to live your covenants, but being around your friends and in a world that has remained the same may make you wonder if you made the right choice by joining the Church. You're not alone in these feelings. Even those of us lucky enough to be raised in the gospel struggle at times. It's difficult to be different. Many times this is what pulls even the strongest member away from the gospel. It is important as a member of the Church to surround yourself with people who live the gospel standards or who live in such a way as to be a good influence and support for you.

Bishop Robert D. Hales said:

"Do you know how to recognize a true friend? A real friend loves us and protects us. In recognizing a true friend, we must look for two important elements in that friendship. A true friend makes it easier for us to live the gospel by being around him. Similarly, a true friend does not make us choose between his way and the Lord's way. A true friend will help us return [to our Heavenly Father] with honor."[3]

You do not have to eliminate all of your old friends and acquaintances from your life; however, living the gospel is easier if you develop a group of friends within the Church or others who live similar standards. These friendships will also help you to increase your knowledge of the gospel as you spend time together. The Church is a wonderful place to meet friends who will encourage your efforts to live the gospel, share common interests and ideas, and allow you to express questions about your new church and lifestyle. Membership in the Church provides a group of almost ready-made friends if you are open to these friendships.

I spent nineteen years of my life living in the same house. That can be very comforting to a child and even a young adult. I think this may be the main reason I'm not fond of change. In fact, I hate it! My husband is almost the polar opposite. As a child, he moved more than fifteen times in eighteen years. I blame this for his ability to embrace change—or at least not hate it as much as I do. In the seventeen years we have been married, we've moved seven times. Only three of those times were to different towns, but since we've changed houses seven times and everything has to go into boxes and be moved, it counts as a move in my book! I realize for most people that probably won't sound like a lot, but for someone who lived in the same house until leaving for college, it is plenty!

In December 2002, our family moved from Montana to southern Idaho. Other than the years I attended university, this was the farthest from my childhood home that I had ever lived. At the time, my two youngest boys were two and three years old, so I was not working outside of our home. I did not know anyone in the small town we moved into. The first few weeks in Emmett were miserable for me as I tried to get used to living away from my family and friends. As the days passed without a friend, I began to doubt that our move had been the best thing for our family, or at least for me.

The first Sunday in Idaho, we attended the blessing of my new niece, Josie, at the ward in Meridian. The second Sunday, our entire family was sick with the stomach flu, so again we were unable to attend our new ward. It was our third week in Idaho when we finally attended our ward. It was then that things began to improve for me. When the Relief Society sisters found out that we were new in town, they sprang into action.

We were renting while we built our new home, and because of this we were driving our two older boys to the school within the boundaries of our new home. Coincidentally, not one block away was a member family who were not only as new to the area as we were but were also building in the very same subdivision outside of town. In addition, they had three kids almost identical in age to our three oldest boys. Within a couple of hours of arriving home from Church that Sunday, our phone rang. My Relief Society sister and new neighbor was calling to arrange a carpool for our kids.

Before the week was out, Kim and I were well on the way to becoming friends. That same week, the Relief Society presidency arrived with a welcome basket, ward list, visiting teaching assignment, and the phone numbers of both our home and visiting teachers. Within a very short period of time I had sisters chatting with me at Church and at my boys' sports events. I had sisters calling to set up play dates with my two little ones at home. My entire family had been reached out to in love and friendship.

By the time we moved back to Montana, I had more close friends whom I loved like true sisters than I had ever had in my life. My time spent in Idaho could have continued to be a miserable experience. Most probably it would have been miserable if it had not been for my membership and almost built-in friendships that are a part of belonging to the Church.

Keep your old friends if they support and uplift you in the new life you have chosen, but look for opportunities to build new friendships within the circle of your brothers and sisters in the gospel. President Thomas S. Monson said:

"We tend to become like those whom we admire . . . and they are usually our friends. Associate with those who, like you, are planning not for temporary convenience, shallow goals, or narrow ambition, but rather for those things that matter most—even eternal objectives."[4]

Just like good, wholesome friends can help protect you from the potholes in your journey on earth, so too can learning to avoid the worldly entertainment that is designed to betray the values and virtue of members of the Church. Avoiding this kind of entertainment can sometimes feel like trying not to get wet in a rainstorm without an umbrella—practically impossible! If you consider the programs on the major networks' prime-time lineups, it is almost impossible to find a program that doesn't glorify the values of the world and mock the wholesome values of Christianity. There are shows that depict homosexuality as a natural, acceptable lifestyle choice; shows that have unmarried couples raising families; and shows that make excessive immorality appear acceptable, and almost every show makes a mockery of the Word of Wisdom. Even sporting events are sponsored by inappropriate products and have commercials that glamorize the use of these products. Most shocking to me as a parent are the animated cartoons that carry adult content and encourage disrespect and vulgarity toward parents and others in authority.

What then is a new member of the Church to do? The thirteenth article of faith says: "If there is anything virtuous, lovely, or of good report or praiseworthy, we seek after these things." It can be very difficult to adjust your viewing habits, but it can be done. That's the wonderful thing about being here on earth—you have agency. You have the ability to choose how you spend your time. You can choose to spend it doing things that could damage your spirituality or spend it living your life to embrace the gospel. It will take persistence and commitment to change what you watch. You may even have periods where you falter in your commitment, but you have the ability to change the channel or turn the TV off. It's a matter of personal moral discipline. D. Todd Christofferson said, "Moral discipline is the consistent exercise of agency to choose the right because it is right, even when it is hard."[5]

Not only does television endorse the values of the world, but so do many movies. Gone are the days when movies received an R rating for the use of curse words. Gone are the days when nudity in a movie required a parent to attend with their child. Rarely do theatres even check to verify the age of youth before they willingly sell them a ticket to a movie. It seems that the morals and values are sold for the price of admissions and a bucket of popcorn.

I can remember the first PG (parental guidance) movie my older sister, our friends, and I tried to attend without an adult. I was in the eleventh grade and was sixteen years old. We had seen the previews and eagerly awaited the arrival of the movie to our hometown theatre. Because we lived in a small town, movies took a lot longer to arrive than at the big city theatres. The wait seemed endless to our teenage minds. Finally, our much anticipated movie had arrived.

A group of us had it all planned—we didn't have a sports game on that Friday night, so that would be the night we'd go to the movie. Since my older sister had her driver's license and a couple of her friends wanted to see the movie too, she would be our chauffeur. We begged our parents for the car: a Buick station wagon with faux wood paneling down the sides. (A lot of my best and most embarrassing childhood memories revolve around that car.) We got the car, and off we headed for the forty-five-minute drive to town.

We arrived a few minutes before the start of the movie. We stepped up to the ticket window and confidently requested tickets to see *Footloose*. To our surprise and teenage disgust, the woman at the window asked where our parents were. We were shocked. We were in the eleventh and twelfth grades. We were high school students, not little kids. The nerve of that woman. No matter what we said or how aggressively we begged, the woman made it very clear we were *not* getting into that movie without a parent.

Back into the Buick we climbed, and home we went, disappointed and disgusted by the "stupid" rule that had kept us out of the movie. Our parents were certainly surprised by our early arrival home. The following evening, Mom drove us all back into town and was our guarantee of admission into the movie. If you ask her about the movie, even though it's been over twenty years, she'll still tell you *Footloose* is one of her favorite movies—mine too!

Now that I'm a parent and have teenage children, I'd give anything to have a theatre ticket agent refuse to sell my boys a ticket to see a movie they shouldn't see. Shan and I are careful not to have any inappropriate movies in our home. We don't rent them and refuse to allow our boys to attend them. Unfortunately, not many other people outside the Church have the same standards, and policing the movies our boys watch has become almost a full-time job. Too often, my teens will say, "Oh, Mom, it's a good movie except for one part." Again and again we are told that Satan doesn't drag us down to hell in one giant heave; it's the little tugs slowly over time—the "except fors"—that are our downfall.

Elder Cree-L Kofford of the Seventy said: "We want to rationalize. I don't know where that is more evident than in watching movies. Young people know they should not watch R- or X-rated movies, and yet time after time I hear them say, 'Well it's only rated R because it's violent.' What difference does it make why it is rated R? The fact is, a prophet of God has said not to go to R-rated movies. That ought to be good enough."[6]

The world has clearly made a wrong turn somewhere along the road of morals and virtue. As a member of the Church, you'll experience many incidents where a movie violates your standards. You have the ability to change the channel on your television or turn off the TV altogether, so you don't have to watch—you can choose virtue over vice.

My husband and I try to go on frequent date nights. With four busy boys, it doesn't happen as often as we'd like. On one such date, we decided to see a movie. I can't remember which movie it was, but I do know that it wasn't R-rated because we committed years and years ago that we wouldn't watch those. The movie began, and within the first few scenes, we were subjected to nudity, profanity, and crude and sexual humor. As I shifted uncomfortably in my seat, I happened to glance over at Shan and was pleased to see that he was as unimpressed with our movie choice as I was. As if sensing my discomfort, he asked if I would like to leave. I was halfway down the stairs in the theater before my answer was out of my mouth!

Despite the fact that this was our evening out and we had paid a lot to get into the movie and to have treats to munch on, we left. We spent the drive home visiting and reaffirming our commitment to love the gospel standards and to diligently teach them to our boys. Years later, I'm grateful to have a husband who was willing to walk out when our values were being attacked. I'm grateful he's that kind of a man!

The worldly values on our televisions and in movies are also imbedded in the music we listen to. With the invention of satellite radio and music download sites on the Internet, every imaginable type of music is available to us and to our children. The content of much of it has become so alarming and disturbing that I even have a hard time listening to the radio on long drives to town. Unclean content has become so commonplace that our children may not even realize what they're listening to. They sing along to the music and seem to be oblivious to the song's content and language and the lifestyles promoted in the songs. Many times I've blown my top about the language in the songs, and my oldest remarks that he didn't even realize there were curse words in the song! Do we realize our values are being eroded as we listen?

In the pamphlet *For the Strength of Youth*, we're told:

> Music is an important and powerful part of life. It can be an influence for good that helps you draw closer to Heavenly Father. However, it can also be used for wicked purposes. Unworthy music may seem harmless, but it can have evil effects on your mind and spirit.
>
> Choose carefully the music you listen to. Pay attention to how you feel when you are listening. Don't listen to music that drives away the Spirit, encourages immorality, glorifies violence, uses foul or offensive language, or promotes Satanism or other evil practices.[7]

Choose carefully what enters your mind, for once it is there, it can be almost impossible to eliminate!

One area of the world that is perhaps the most dangerous to our values and virtues is the Internet. What a wonderful invention it is! We can communicate with people around the world without ever leaving home. With the click of a few keys, all the information in the entire world is at our fingertips. Unfortunately, so is all the other trash the world has to offer. With the creation of the Internet, we welcome evil right into our homes and families. No longer do we have to leave home to find it.

> A computer and a telephone line provide the doorway to an online world of libraries, museums, businesses, schools, and, most of all, people—people all over the world willing to talk to you. . . . The Internet is an exciting place.
>
> However, parts of that online world are dangerous. Some Internet neighborhoods attract people and businesses you and your family need to avoid. Some people will want to steal your money and threaten your safety. Without parental guidance and supervision,

children can put themselves in physical danger or encounter materials that are spiritual and intellectual poison.[8]

I can remember a time, not that long ago, when pornographic magazines were wrapped in plain brown wrappers with only the name of the magazine on the outside. These magazines were then placed out of reach behind the counter of the stores that chose to sell them. Anyone who wished to purchase that garbage actually had to ask the store clerk to get it for them. They had to let someone else know what they were looking at and what they lacked in moral values. They could not purchase it without others knowing about their desire for the filth. That isn't the case anymore.

Elder Russell M. Ballard spoke at a commencement address at Brigham Young University—Hawaii in December 2007. He said:

> Today we have a modern equivalent of the printing press in the Internet. The Internet allows everyone to be a publisher, to have his or her voice heard, and it is revolutionizing society. . . . The emergence of new media is facilitating a worldwide conversation on almost every subject, including religion, and nearly everyone can participate. This modern equivalent of the printing press is not reserved only for the elite.
>
> Now some of these tools—like any tool in an unpracticed or undisciplined hand—can be dangerous. The Internet can be used to proclaim the gospel of Jesus Christ and can just as easily be used to market the filth and sleaze of pornography. . . . Satan is always quick to exploit the negative power of new inventions, to spoil and degrade, and to neutralize any effect for good. Make sure that the choices you make in the use of new media are choices that expand your mind, increase your opportunities, and feed your soul."[9]

Access to any kind of vulgar image or disturbing video sits in our own homes on our personal computers. One quick Internet search will allow you to find any kind of exploitative pornography you may want. No one has to know what you're looking at—the searcher is a nameless, faceless surfer on the web. The Internet can't tell whether the viewer is a forty-year-old, single man, a married father, or a ten-year-old boy who has clicked the wrong link. What a dangerous lack of personal accountability! Even more disturbing is that you don't even have to go searching for it—the evils of the Internet will find you.

We have been diligent in following the counsel given by Church leaders with regard to the Internet. "Parents need to make online use a family, not a private, activity. Put the computer in a room that the whole family uses, not in a child's bedroom. Be aware of when and how your child uses the computer. Take time to learn how to use the Internet yourself. This can help make you aware of what your child is doing and will give you the vocabulary you need to talk to your child about the Internet."[10]

Our computer is in the home office connected to the kitchen, which, with four growing boys, is the busiest room in our home! We regularly check the computer history and our children's networking accounts. We have filters on our content, and our Internet service provider has additional filters to prevent pop-ups from attacking our computer. I thought we were well protected. It's interesting how Satan works. He waits until we feel secure about something or until we let our guard down—then he strikes.

I sat down at my computer a few weeks ago and scanned in an old picture of my husband from his youth (a very old picture!). As I waited for the picture to load, I happened to glance at the picture folders on my computer window. Something in the "sample pictures" folder caught my attention, and I opened the file. To my surprise and complete disgust, there were approximately thirty inappropriate photos on my computer! Not only were the pictures on my computer, but also Internet links to the websites where they had originated!

A quick check into the computer history, the hard drive, and the pictures' properties allowed me to find that this filth had been loaded onto my computer at a time when our entire family was away from home, either at work or at school. A bit more investigating, and I found that I was responsible for this download of trash. I had mistakenly left my Internet link connected one morning after having checked the news and weather forecast. That's all it took—a few hours of unmonitored, uninterrupted Internet access—for that garbage to be loaded by some company onto my computer. My computer—where my boys and husband could easily have seen it and unwittingly accessed much more!

"Sadly, the best filters made will not ensure that nothing profane will enter our homes. While the Internet is wonderful, we must be vigilant regarding it and other media influences in the home. Pornography is becoming all too prevalent and is seeping into the lives of Saints, turning their hearts away from the standards of God."[11]

Dieter F. Uchtdorf, Second Counselor in the First Presidency, counseled us about the Internet when he said:

"Be cautious. These same technologies can allow evil influences to cross the threshold of your homes. These dangerous traps are only a mouse click away. Pornography, violence, intolerance, and ungodliness destroy families, marriages, and individual lives. These dangers are distributed through many media, including magazines, books, television, movies, and music, as well as the Internet."[12]

Be careful, be vigilant, be obsessive and paranoid if you have to, but do whatever it takes to keep the evils of the world off your computers and out of your homes!

Have you ever just sat and listened to the people around you? Try it! The next time you're around a group of people, just sit and listen. Don't listen only to what the conversation is about; listen to the language used. It's amazing how people speak and what they waste their time talking about—and most of us don't even realize it.

I'm a substitute teacher in our school district in Montana, and I have a lot of opportunities to sit and listen—it's actually one of my tactics to find out what is going on in the schools my boys attend. Sneaky, I know, but it works. I'm amazed by the language used, from the elementary school kids all the way up through the staff! Students as young as the first grade frequently use the Lord's name in vain, and when I bring it to their attention, they are completely unaware of what they said wrong. For the older students and even staff members, curse words are no longer reserved for rare moments of anger and frustration but are common conversational words.

It's interesting that while the little children don't realize that what they're saying is wrong, most high school students will apologize for their inappropriate language when I ask them to watch their language or tell them I'm offended when they use the Lord's name that way. When we're not careful about the words we choose, we can easily fall into the habit of using worldly, inappropriate language.

Growing up, my mom always told us that people who cursed were just not smart enough to think of a different word to use. I can still remember the first time one of us girls was stupid enough to swear at home.

We had a walk-out basement under our home, and because Dad was always busy working on something else, the deck off the main floor living room took years to build. We had a back door that led out to where the deck would have been, but instead of the deck was a four-foot drop to the rocky ground below. Going in and out of that door was possible, but not an easy task. On hot summer days, the back door was often left open to allow a breeze to blow through the house. One afternoon, my older sister, Bonnie, was standing, looking out the door. Our friend Sarann was spending the week with us and saw Bonnie standing in the opening. It was too big of a temptation to ignore. With one small push, Sarann sent Bonnie sprawling into the great abyss. As Bonnie hit the ground in a dusty pile, she let a curse word escape. Within seconds, Mom had made a mad dash up from the laundry room in the basement. I remember that it was a fast trial and that the principle of guilt by association was applied. All of us spent most of that bright, sunny, summer day sitting on the couch, in trouble.

President Gordon B. Hinckley counseled:

> Even among *our* young people, there is an evil and growing habit of profanity and the use of foul and filthy language. . . .
>
> . . . Stay out of the gutter in your conversation. Foul talk defiles the man who speaks it.
>
> If you have the habit, how do you break it? You begin by making a decision to change. The next time you are prone to use words you know to be wrong, simply stop. Keep quiet or say what you have to say in a different way. As you practice such restraint, it will become easy. . . .
>
> . . . Conversation is the substance of friendly social activity. It can be happy. It can be light. It can be earnest. It can be funny. But it must not be salty, or uncouth, or foul if one is in sincerity a believer in Christ. . . .
>
> Don't swear. Don't profane. Avoid so-called dirty jokes. Stay away from conversation that is sprinkled with foul and filthy words. You will be happier if you do so, and your example will give strength to others.[2]

Watch your language! The way you speak and what you speak about says a lot about you. If you were sensible enough to join the Church, you're smart enough to come up with another word to use. Make that your habit.

It takes hard work and dedication to live in the world without becoming overcome by the world. Sometimes it may seem that despite your best efforts, it is impossible to isolate yourself from all the evils and temptations in the world. While this is true, you *can* live the gospel and keep your baptismal covenants. How you do it and the success you have depend largely on your attitude and efforts to avoid the influences of the world and stay close to the gospel.

The world is like a rough road filled with potholes and mud puddles. They are around every corner and can be found in every road. Some are out in the open—easy to see and easy to avoid. Others are hidden in the dips in the road or on the unnoticed edges of the pavement. These are much harder to avoid. The evils of the world are like that. Sometimes they are big and out in the open and easy to avoid. Other temptations are hidden in the low spots in our lives or near the edge of something that seems to be good. Just like a mud puddle in the road that you have to go through, you have to live through the trials and influences of the world. You can go splashing and stomping through them without a care for how dirty you get or how difficult it will be to get clean or you can go cautiously, carefully, and deliberately through, all the while looking for safe places to step so as to avoid the mud and filth. No matter how you go through the puddle, there will be consequences on the other side depending on how dirty you've become. Stay out of the mud and stay as clean as you possibly can! Your eternal happiness depends on it.

It won't be easy—nothing important ever is—but following the guidelines given will make this so much less challenging. As is counseled in *For the Strength of Youth*:

> Do not attend, view, or participate in entertainment that is vulgar, immoral, violent, or pornographic in any way. Do not participate in entertainment that in any way presents immorality or violent behavior as acceptable. . . .
>
> Have the courage to walk out of a movie or video party, turn off a computer or television, change a radio station, or put down a magazine if what is being presented does not meet Heavenly Father's standards. Do these things even if others do not.[13]

NOTES

1. James E. Faust, "The Power to Change," *Ensign*, Nov. 2007, 122–24.
2. Gordon B. Hinckley, "Take Not the Name of God in Vain," *Ensign*, Nov. 1987, 44.
3. "They Spoke to Us," *Friend*, June 1990, 5.

4. Thomas S. Monson, "The Lighthouse of the Lord: A Message to the Youth of the Church," *New Era*, Feb. 2001, 2.
5. D. Todd Christofferson, "Moral Discipline," *Ensign*, Nov. 2009, 105–8.
6. Cree-L Kofford, "Marriage in the Lord's Way, Part Two," *Ensign*, July 1998, 15.
7. "Music and Dancing," *For the Strength of Youth: Fulfilling Our Duty to God* (Salt Lake City: Intellectual Reserve, 2001), 20.
8. William C. Porter, "I Have a Question," *Ensign*, Mar. 2001, 58–59.
9. M. Russell Ballard, from a commencement address given at Brigham Young University—Hawaii on December 15, 2007.
10. William C. Porter, "I Have a Question," *Ensign*, Mar. 2001, 58–59.
11. Kathleen H. Hughes, "Blessing Our Families through Our Covenants," *Ensign*, Nov. 2002, 106.
12. Dieter F. Uchtdorf, "A Matter of a Few Degrees," *Ensign*, May 2008, 57–60.
13. "Entertainment and the Media," *For the Strength of Youth: Fulfilling Our Duty to God* (Salt Lake City: Intellectual Reserve, 2001), 17, 19.

8 Arriving Home Safely

Getting Back in One Piece

"There's nothing half so pleasant as coming home again."
Margaret Elizabeth Sangster

There is no place I love as much as home. Even as a grown woman with children of my own, I still get a special feeling each time I see the roof of my parents' home as we drive to visit them. It is a feeling that all will be well as soon as I am within the circle of their love again. I can only imagine that this must be a mere fragment of what we will feel as we return to our heavenly parents at the conclusion of our earthly life. Our happiness at the reunion will, however, depend on how we've lived while here on earth.

You've made an important and wonderful step by joining The Church of Jesus Christ of Latter-day Saints. As you've read, I hope you have come to realize that your baptism was only the first step in a long journey. Each step you take from that day until the day of your final step on earth will determine how you will feel when you arrive at your heavenly home. Will you anticipate the reunion with dread because of the poor choices you made here on earth, or will you eagerly await the blessed opportunity to be joyfully reunited with your loved ones?

Elder Robert D. Hales of the Quorum of the Twelve shared an experience with regard to this:

> As a young man, I had an opportunity to serve in the U.S. Air Force as a jet fighter pilot. Each unit in the 308th Fighter Bomber Squadron had a motto to inspire their efforts. Our motto, "Return with Honor," graced the side of our fighter aircraft. "Return with Honor" was a constant reminder to us of our determination to return to our home base with honor only after having expended all of our efforts to successfully complete every aspect of our mission.

> This same motto, "Return with Honor," can be applied to each of us on our eternal path of progression. Having lived with our Heavenly Father and having come to earth, we must have determination to return with honor to our heavenly home.[1]

As you grow in knowledge and testimony of the gospel, this strange world and culture that come with your membership in The Church of Jesus Christ of Latter-day Saints will become as familiar and comforting as the driveway to your own home. I hope your journey through life will be blessed as you strive to live the gospel of Jesus Christ. Choose your path with unfailing faith in your Lord and Savior. Allow your membership in the Church to uplift, support, and guide you. As with any journey, this mortal life will be so much easier with help and guidance, which your membership in the Church can provide for you.

Time passes quickly, and before long, you'll no longer need a road map. You'll become one of the guides giving directions and assistance to new members. Find peace in the knowledge that no matter how long we've been members of the Church, each of us started where you are—at the beginning. Embrace the gospel and rejoice in the blessings it brings to you and to your family—they are eternal.

When times become difficult and things seem hopeless, look to your leaders, friends, and family in the gospel for help, support, and comfort. Find faith in the words of Elder Dieter F. Uchtdorf:

> Enduring to the end is a process filling every minute of our life, every hour, every day, from sunrise to sunrise. It is accomplished through personal discipline following the commandments of God.
>
> The restored gospel of Jesus Christ is a way of life. It is not for Sunday only. It is not something we can do only as a habit or a tradition if we expect to harvest all of its promised blessings.
>
> My dear brothers and sisters, there will be days and nights when you feel overwhelmed, when your hearts are heavy and your heads hang down. Then, please remember, Jesus Christ, the Redeemer, is the Head of this Church. It is His gospel. He wants you to succeed. He gave His life for just this purpose. He is the Son of the living God.[2]

I pray that each of you may gain some help and guidance from the counsel, experiences, and stories shared within the pages of this book. May you continue to study, pray, and grow in the gospel through your membership in this wonderful church. Enjoy the journey!

NOTES

1. Robert D. Hales, "Return with Honor," *New Era*, Nov. 2001, 10.
2. Dieter F. Uchtdorf, "Have We Not Reason to Rejoice?," *Ensign*, Nov. 2007, 18–21.

APPENDIX

HELP! I NEED A TRANSLATOR!

UNDERSTANDING THE LANGUAGE OF THE CHURCH

> *"A different language is a different vision of life."*
> ***Federico Fellini***

Seventeen years ago, my desperate and clueless husband was foolish enough to ask me to marry him—and as his luck would have it, I said yes. The poor guy was quickly submersed in what can only be described as a crazy family. In our family, quoting Disney movies is not only a habit, but almost essential to communicate with each other. In addition to the theft of ideas from Disney, my family has what my husband refers to as a language all our own. We refer often to made-up words from our childhood and mispronunciations of words from younger siblings as though everyone in the world should understand. For example, a *mic-pic-tabbie* is well known in my family to mean a picnic table, thanks to the inability of my sister Novalee to speak clearly as a three- or four-year-old. Potatoes are *pottlebees,* thanks to my over-anxiousness in reading in the third grade. Needless to say, people new to our family have quite a hard time understanding us when we all get together!

Similarly, as new members of the Church, converts may find themselves having a difficult—if not impossible—time understanding many of the conversations, announcements, and talks that occur as experienced members rattle away. Within your first few days as a new member or maybe even earlier, you probably heard people talk about CTR rings or the D&C, not to mention the rivalry between BYU and the U. Were you a bit confused when you overheard someone talking about how excited their daughter was at Mutual to find out that a branch member's son had left the MTC and was in the mission field?

You probably didn't even know the Church had fields! You may have wondered why the bishop has a storehouse and why someone is asking you how much food you have stored in your home. All these abbreviations and phrases are probably as unfamiliar to you as they would be if they were spoken in French, Spanish, or even Latin.

A brief list of some of the jargon and abbreviations you'll hear on a regular basis may help. This is by no means the entire list of LDS terms. (See, there's an abbreviation already!) Think of this chapter as a kind of traveler's condensed version of a foreign language. You may want to refer to this list when you come across a word or phrase you don't understand or haven't heard before.

Let's get started, since we have a long list to cover!

Aaronic Priesthood: The lesser, or preparatory, priesthood, which contains the offices of deacon, teacher, priest, and bishop. Church brethren who hold this priesthood serve primarily as stewards of the temporal (earthly) affairs of the Church and can also perform baptisms and administer the sacrament. It also helps male members of the Church become ready to enter into additional covenants. New converts and young men who are at least twelve years old and who are worthy are ordained to this priesthood.

active in the Church: This refers to a member who regularly attends their Church meetings, lives the gospel principles and teachings, and is willing to accept callings within the Church.

administer: To perform a religious ordinance, such as saying the prayers to bless the sacrament. You'll often hear the person conducting the meeting thank the members of the Aaronic Priesthood for administering the sacrament.

agency: This is the ability to choose. You may sometimes hear people refer to it as "free" agency. However, it is not free. Christ suffered and died for our sins and paid the price for us to have this agency. While we have the agency to choose whether we will make good or evil choices, we do not have the ability to choose the consequences of those choices.

Articles of Faith: The thirteen basic beliefs of The Church of Jesus Christ of Latter-day Saints. These are found in the Pearl of Great Price. They were written by the first prophet of the restored Church,

Joseph Smith. Children are encouraged to memorize them while in Primary. Many of the pass-along cards given out by the missionaries contain the Articles of Faith. Most of the articles begin with the phrase "We believe."

AP: An abbreviation for either the Aaronic Priesthood (see above) or the assistant to the president. The assistant to the president is a counselor to the president of the various auxiliaries. "But whether it be a bishopric, stake presidency, Aaronic or Melchizedek priesthood quorum presidency, mission presidency, temple presidency, auxiliary organization presidency, Area Presidency, or the First Presidency of the Church, there is a president with counselors."[1]

Apostle: Each of the twelve priesthood leaders of the Church who serve as special witnesses of Christ and assistants to the president of the Church, just as the twelve apostles of Jesus did in the ancient world. As one member of the Quorum of the Twelve Apostles dies, another Apostle is called in his place. An Apostle holds the Melchizedek, or higher, priesthood.

auxiliary: The organizations of the Church, which includes Primary, Relief Society, Sunday School, Young Men, and Young Women groups. Each auxiliary has a leadership group that reports to the bishopric or branch presidency.

baptisms for the dead: A sacred temple ordinance in which worthy members of the Church perform vicarious baptisms in the temple for people who have died. Members of the Church must be at least twelve years of age, be interviewed by a member of the bishopric or branch presidency, and receive a special use temple recommend to perform this ordinance.

bishop: Sometimes capitalized. The priesthood leader of a local congregation known as a ward. Members of the ward refer to him as Bishop (last name of the leader), for example: Bishop Smith. The office of bishop is the highest office found within the Aaronic Priesthood. The bishop is responsible for overseeing the affairs of the Church on a local level.

Book of Mormon (BoM): This is a part of the holy scriptures used by members of The Church of Jesus Christ of Latter-day Saints. It is another testament of Jesus Christ and was translated by Joseph Smith from the gold plates. It contains a record of the peoples of the American continent and includes their history and the sacred writings of the prophets in the Americas.

born in the covenant (BIC): This refers to children born to members who have been sealed to each other in the temple ceremony.

branch: A small unit of Church members.

branch council: A monthly meeting involving the branch president and the leaders of the various auxiliaries in which the needs, upcoming activities, and issues of each organization are discussed.

branch president: This is the priesthood leader who presides over a small local congregation known as a branch. He is referred to as President (last name of leader), for example: President Smith. His duties and office are the same as those of a bishop except they are for a smaller group of members.

Brigham Young University (BYU): Located in Provo, Utah, BYU is the largest and oldest of the Church's educational institutions.

> The university traces its roots to Utah's rich pioneer heritage. The original school, Brigham Young Academy, was established Oct. 16, 1875, on a little over one acre of land in what is now downtown Provo. At that time, Brigham Young, president of The Church of Jesus Christ of Latter-day Saints, charged that all secular learning at the institution should be fused with teachings from the scriptures.
>
> Speaking to Academy Principal Karl G. Maeser, President Young said: "Brother Maeser, I want you to remember that you ought not to teach even the alphabet or the multiplication tables without the Spirit of God."
>
> BYU has remained true to that original charge. With the help and sacrifice of Abraham O. Smoot, the campus moved in 1891 to new facilities on University Avenue. The Academy's curriculum strengthened and enrollment grew. In 1903, the name was officially changed to Brigham Young University. With the help of its committed presidents, BYU has continued to grow, refine its mission and pursue excellence in all areas.[2]

From its humble beginning, BYU has grown to be the third largest privately owned university in the United States, with an enrollment in 2009 in excess of 32,000 students.

brother or sister: Sometimes capitalized. Members of the Church often refer to the members of the Church by the designation of brother or sister as a reference to the fact that we are all sons and daughters of our Heavenly Father and therefore, brothers and sisters in the gospel. For example, at church my husband is referred to as Brother Davis and I would be Sister Davis. The word *sister* when referring to a female missionary is a title for her calling.

calling: An invitation issued to a member of the Church to accept an office, assignment, or responsibility within the Church. This may include being a teacher of gospel doctrine for adults, youth, or children of the Church, a visiting teacher, or even a nursery worker. Whatever calling is extended to you, it is helpful to know that there are no small callings in the Church and each one comes from the Lord. As mentioned earlier, Elder Henry B. Eyring taught: "You are called of God. The Lord knows you. He knows whom He would have serve in every position in His Church. He chose you."[3]

chapel: The room in the meetinghouse (church) where sacrament meetings and other sacred meetings are conducted. Members should dress and conduct themselves appropriately for attendance within the chapel.

choose the right (CTR): This is a motto taught to children in Primary and reinforced throughout all gospel teachings. It is to serve as a reminder to always make good choices. The symbol is found on a variety of items, the most common being the CTR ring.

church: Sometimes capitalized. The common term used by members to refer to both the buildings where services are held as well as a short version of the official name of The Church of Jesus Christ of Latter-day Saints.

Church Educational System (CES): Includes many varying institutions that provide both religious and secular education at the elementary, secondary, and postsecondary levels and to adult learners. "Approximately 1.2 million individuals were enrolled in CES programs in approximately 135 countries during the 2003–2004 school year. CES courses of study are separate and distinct from religious instruction provided through LDS Church congregations."[4]

convert: An individual who believes the doctrine taught, has chosen to be baptized and confirmed a member, and commits his life to living the gospel of Jesus Christ.

covenant: A two-way promise with the Lord in which we promise to do something or live a principle and in exchange the Lord promises to bless us for our obedience.

deacon: The first office in the Aaronic Priesthood. Members of this office are male Church members who are usually between the ages of twelve and fourteen. They are the sharply dressed young men who usually pass the sacrament to the congregation on Sundays.

degrees of glory: The kingdoms of heaven, which include the telestial, terrestrial, and celestial kingdoms.

distribution center: A facility where Church members can go to purchase Church publications and other supplies related to the Church. You may have a distribution center near you. If not, you may order from them by mail, phone, or the Internet and have your order shipped to you.

district: A group of several units called branches.

Doctrine and Covenants (D&C): An additional book of scriptures used in the Church. It contains revelations and writings received through Joseph Smith and other leaders of the Church. The chapters in the Doctrine and Covenants are referred to as sections.

Duty to God: A program within the Young Men organization in which the young men are encouraged and assisted in setting and keeping goals that will benefit their future lives as priesthood leaders within their homes, their communities, and the Church.

elder: Sometimes capitalized. An office in the Melchizedek Priesthood. It is also used to refer to male missionaries and General Authorities.

***Ensign*:** A monthly Church publication for adult members of the Church that includes articles, talks, and messages approved by the General Authorities of the Church.

elders quorum (EQ): A group of men within the Melchizedek Priesthood who hold the office of elder.

elders quorum president (EQP): The leader of the elders quorum.

endowment: A sacred ordinance performed only within the walls of a temple of the Church, in which a worthy member of the Church receives guidance and instruction on living the gospel and makes covenants with the Lord.

enrichment: Monthly week-night meetings for the adult female members of the Church. The full name of the meeting was "home, family, and personal enrichment meeting." The name was changed in October 2009 to "Relief Society meeting," but it may take some time for units to transition away from calling it an enrichment meeting.

Especially for Youth (EFY): A special multiday, overnight program that brings together the youth of the Church and their friends in a Christian atmosphere of fun and fellowship. "Youth have the opportunity to learn and grow together while attending classes, devotionals, and firesides together. Weekly highlights include Family Home Evening, dances, a musical program, games night, service projects, a variety show, good food, and a testimony meeting. Added benefits are new friendships, strengthened testimonies, and lasting memories."[5]

Faith in God: The Primary program designed for boys and girls aged eight and over to help them develop habits that encourage them to live the gospel standards, build their testimonies, and resist temptation. An important part of the Faith in God program is keeping your baptismal covenant and staying spiritually strong. By fulfilling the requirements before their twelfth birthday, children can earn an award.

Family Home Evening (FHE): A program within the Church in which family members gather together once a week, usually on a Monday evening, to learn, play, and grow together as a family. The Church has lesson manuals for Family Home Evening, which can be accessed online at the Church website, www.lds.org, or purchased from the distribution center.

fast Sunday: Usually on the first Sunday of each month, members of the Church are asked to go without food or drink for two meals and donate the money saved from this "fast" to the Church to help provide assistance for those in need. During sacrament meeting, called fast and testimony meeting on this Sunday, members are invited and encouraged to bear their testimonies of the gospel to the congregation.

fellowship: to treat someone as a friend and show genuine care and concern for his involvement in the Church and to show genuine interest in his life.

firesides: Gatherings of Church members and guests that highlight a special speaker or program of a spiritual theme. A variety of firesides throughout the year are Churchwide and may be broadcast to local buildings. Some firesides are specific to a particular group in the Church—for example, there may be a fireside on dating that is for the youth of the Church and their parents.

First Presidency: The President of the Church and his counselors.

food storage: a supply of food and provisions such as medicine, money, and the necessities of life that can sustain you for a period of time. The leadership of the Church advises that, where possible, each member should have at least three months' worth of necessities stored.

***Friend*:** A monthly Church magazine for the children of the Church.

garments: Sacred underclothing that is worn by members of the Church who have gone to the temple and participated in the endowment ordinance.

General Authorities: Members of the presiding leadership of the Church. These include members of the First Presidency, Quorum of the Twelve Apostles, Quorums of the Seventy, and Presiding Bishopric.

general conference: A biannual meeting for the entire membership of the Church. These meetings are held in Salt Lake City, Utah, in April and October of each year. They are broadcast to local units and can be viewed on the official Church website. The talks given in these meetings are published the following month in the *Ensign*, one of the Church magazines. You may also order copies of the talks on CD or DVD from the distribution center.

high council: A group of twelve priesthood members in the stake who hold the office of high priest. This group helps direct the affairs of the Church on a stake level.

high priest: An office in the Melchizedek Priesthood.

Holy Ghost: The third member of the Godhead, who is a personage without flesh and blood and is a spirit. He is also referred to as the "Comforter."

home teachers and home teaching (HT): Each family on the membership records of the Church is assigned two priesthood holders to visit them on a monthly basis to fellowship them and assist them with any concerns or temporal needs the family may have.

initiatory: The initial temple ordinance a worthy member will perform in the temple. The initiatory consists of the ceremonial washing and anointing in preparation for the endowment.

institute: Religious instruction for students who are attending colleges, universities, or postsecondary schools. It is also for young single adults who live within the same boundaries as the institute. The term refers to the class instruction as well as to the building in which it is held. This program of the Church is under the direction of the CES.

investigator: This term is used to refer to someone who is interested in learning about The Church of Jesus Christ of Latter-day Saints and is actively meeting with the missionaries.

Joseph Smith Translation (JST): This is Joseph Smith's translation of the Bible. It is found in footnotes and in the Pearl of Great Price.

keys of the priesthood: The divine authority given to men to exercise or direct the ordinances of the gospel and to preside over or lead the various quorums, auxiliaries, and general organization of the Church.

King James Version (KJV): The version of the Bible accepted by the Church to be the most correctly translated version of the original ancient text to English.

Latter-day Saints (LDS): This term is often short for The Church of Jesus Christ of Latter-day Saints.

Melchizedek Priesthood (MP): The higher, or secondary, priesthood, which includes the offices of elder, Seventy, high priest, patriarch, and Apostle. This priesthood focuses on the spiritual matters of the Church.

mission: A term used to refer to a specific geographic region of the world whether there is a Church unit in the area or not. It also refers to a period of voluntary service to the Church and to the group of people called to serve there. Some missions are to share the gospel to nonmembers throughout the world, while others are to offer much needed service in needy nations.

Missionary Training Center (MTC): Special centers where missionaries are trained and taught gospel principles and foreign languages before they leave for their assigned missions.

mission president: The priesthood holder who is given stewardship over a mission and the missionaries who are serving in that area.

Mormon: The informal term used to refer to members of The Church of Jesus Christ of Latter-day Saints. Members are encouraged not to use this term when referring to their religious affiliation.

Mutual: The organization of the Church for youth aged twelve to eighteen.

***New Era*:** A magazine for the youth of the Church published on a monthly basis.

nursery: The Primary class designed for children eighteen months to three years. This should not be looked upon as a babysitting assignment for those called as Nursery workers nor as free child care for parents of small children.

Official Declaration—1: Revelation received in 1890 by President Wilford Woodruff that eliminated the practice of plural marriage from the Church. This declaration is found in the Doctrine and Covenants.

Official Declaration—2: Revelation received in 1978 by President Spencer W. Kimball in which the Lord expressed his will that all worthy male members of the Church who are at least twelve years of age be given the blessing of the priesthood. This declaration is found in the Doctrine and Covenants.

ordinance: A spiritually binding act performed by proper priesthood authority. Some ordinances, such as baptism, may be conducted outside of the temple while others, such as the sealing ordinance, must be performed within the sacred temple.

patriarch: Sometimes capitalized. An office in the Melchizedek Priesthood and also used to refer to the father of a family.

patriarchal blessing: A formal blessing from the Lord given through the ordained Patriarch in which the recipient's lineage from one of the tribes of Israel is revealed in addition to special life instructions and blessings specific to the individual.

priesthood interview: A regular meeting with your priesthood leader in which you have the ability to report on problems, concerns, and issues with your various callings, responsibilities, or duties within the Church. These are conducted monthly, yearly, or as needed depending on your calling and duties within the Church.

Personal Progress: This program is part of the Young Women organization in which the young girls are encouraged and assisted in making and keeping goals that will be beneficial to their spiritual, educational, emotional, physical, and mental well-being.

priesthood: The authority to act in God's name, or the right and responsibility to preside in the Church organization. This term is also used to refer to the men in the Church.

priesthood session: A special meeting held twice each year during general conference that is intended specifically for the members of the priesthood in the Church. The talks given during this meeting are published the following month in the Church magazines so that all members may benefit from the words of Church leaders.

Primary: The Church organization for children aged eighteen months to twelve years. "Our Father in Heaven has given priesthood and Primary leaders the sacred responsibility to help parents teach children the gospel of Jesus Christ and to prepare boys to receive the Aaronic Priesthood and girls to become righteous young women. Through Sunday meetings and weekday activities, the Primary auxiliary helps children learn and live gospel principles; remember and keep their baptismal covenants; and build strong, enduring testimonies."[6]

Proclamation, the: The full name of this document is "The Family: A Proclamation to the World." In this statement presented by President Gordon B. Hinckley at the general Relief Society meeting on September 23, 1995, in Salt Lake City, Utah, the prophets and Apostles testify of the sacred nature of the family as well as the duties and responsibilities of each member of the family.

prophet: Sometimes capitalized. One who holds all the priesthood keys necessary to lead the Lord's Church on the earth. It can also be used to refer to one who has a testimony of Jesus Christ and by the power of the Holy Ghost has received the ability to prophesy.

Quorum of the Twelve Apostles: A group made up of the Apostles of the Church who, under the direction and leadership of the First Presidency, direct the affairs of the Church and act as special witnesses of Jesus Christ.

Quorum of the Seventy: General Authorities who are organized in groups of up to seventy members who, under the direction and leadership of the First Presidency of the Church and the Quorum of the Twelve Apostles, guide the missionary and administrative affairs of the Church.

returned missionary (RM): A member of the Church who has returned with honor from a mission.

Relief Society (RS): The organization of the Church formed for sisters who are eighteen years of age and over. "The Relief Society was founded by the Prophet Joseph Smith on March 17, 1842, in Nauvoo, Illinois. In the days of its founding, it had two main purposes: to provide relief for the poor and needy and to bring people to Christ. The organization continues today, staying true to those original guiding principles as women in the Relief Society meet together on Sunday and in other settings as needed."[7]

sacrament: The religious ordinance in which the bread and water are blessed and passed to the congregation to represent Jesus Christ's body and blood, which he sacrificed for each of us.

sealing: A sacred ordinance performed in the temple in which couples and families have the opportunity to be joined together in their family unit for time and all eternity.

self-reliance: The principle taught by the Church that wherever possible the members of the Church should be responsible for providing for the necessities of themselves and their families.

seminary: A religious course offered to high school students that teaches from the standard works of the Church. In some areas seminary occurs in the morning before school begins, in others your children may have the opportunity to select it as a course in the high school they attend—this is known as released-time seminary. In other smaller areas, seminary may be held once a week, and students are given assignments to complete on the other days of the week. This is known as home-study seminary.

Seventy: An office within the Melchizedek Priesthood that has a special calling to direct missionary and administrative activities within the Church.

splits: An informal word used to refer to times when the missionaries who are serving full-time missions split up their companionship and each goes with a member to their meetings or lessons with investigators. It is important to realize that the elders may only pair up with other adult priesthood holders and sister missionaries will work only with other adult female members of the Church. It is a great opportunity for members of the Church to grab on to the missionary spirit!

sharing time: This is found within the Primary organization and is part of the Sunday block of meetings. During this period, Primary children have the opportunity to sing songs, share scriptures, say prayers, and even give talks to their Primary congregation. Each month the *Friend* magazine contains some ideas for sharing time activities and enhancement.

single adults (SA): Those Church members aged eighteen and over who have graduated from high school but have not yet married. In many areas there are wards established for these members to attend in order to allow them to socialize with other members who share similar life circumstances. The term is sometimes used specifically for single adults thirty-one years old and older.

stake: A group of several wards or a combination of both wards and branches that are in the same geographical area. This group is presided over by a stake president and receives counsel from high councilmen and patriarchs, who do not receive payment for their service.

stake center: The church building in which the administrative offices of the stake officers are located. It is also where most stake meetings and activities are held.

stake president: The priesthood leader who is the presiding authority over the affairs of the stake. He is assisted by counselors and assistants as necessary.

standard works: This term is used to refer to the scriptures used and authorized by The Church of Jesus Christ of Latter-day Saints. They include the King James Version of the Holy Bible, the

Book of Mormon, the Doctrine and Covenants, and the Pearl of Great Price. They may be joined together in a variety of ways; for example, when they are all bound together they are referred to as a "quadruple combination" or "quad," and when the D&C, Book of Mormon, and Pearl of Great Price are bound together they are referred to as the "triple combination."

Sunday dress: At Sunday meetings, men should generally wear a suit or sport coat, white shirt, and tie. Women should wear modest skirts or dresses (with sleeves), and children should be in their very best. Elder D. Todd Christofferson said, "We dress formally at church and other sacred occasions not because we are important, but because the occasion is important."[8]

Sunday dress is also worn when attending the temple. For most Church activities not held on Sunday, casual, modest attire is appropriate. If the activity or meeting is to be held in the chapel, Sunday dress should always be worn so as not to offend the Lord.

Sunday School: An auxiliary in the Church that focuses on teachings related to the scriptures. Each age group in the Church participates in a Sunday School lesson. There may be a variety of Sunday School classes offered depending on the number, needs, and interests of the members of your unit. For example, for new converts, there may be a Gospel Essentials class offered to help you gain further knowledge of the topics you were taught by the missionaries.

teacher: An office in the Aaronic Priesthood. This also refers to any person who presents a lesson.

temple: A sacred building belonging to the Church in which holy ceremonies and ordinances are performed by worthy members of the Church for themselves as well as by proxy for the dead.

temple recommend: A card given to a worthy member of the Church that signifies his worthiness to enter the temple of the Lord. It is given to the member after a personal worthiness interview with both his unit leader (the bishop or branch president) and a member of the stake or district presidency.

***Time Out for Women*:** A Christian women's conference that is held throughout North America. While it does feature speakers, authors, and personalities from the Church, it is not sponsored or endorsed directly by the Church, but rather by Deseret Book, a publishing company owned by the Church.

tithing: A voluntary donation of 10 percent of your income, which is given to the Church as an offering to the Lord and as an expression of gratitude to Him for the many blessings you receive.

University of Utah (the U): Located in Salt Lake City, Utah, the University of Utah is the state's oldest institute of higher education—founded in 1850 as the University of Deseret. Although it is a public university, it has strong ties to many prominent LDS families who both attended the school and contribute through donations to its continued success. The U and BYU have a rivalry that dates back to the earliest athletic competitions and continues to be a source of great debate and excitement. It can be said that you can't like both the U and BYU—you either don't care, or you love one and hate the other! No, that's not very charitable or Christlike, I agree, but it's how some people feel!

visiting teachers and visiting teaching (VT): Similar in structure to home teaching, visiting teaching is part of the Relief Society organization, in which each sister on the records of the Church has the opportunity to receive two other sisters into her home each month to share a religious message and receive fellowship and service.

ward: A term that refers to a large congregation of Saints who meet together. As with branches, stakes, and districts, ward boundaries are determined by the number of members in a geographical area.

ward council: A monthly meeting involving the bishop and the leaders of the various auxiliaries in which the needs, upcoming activities, and issues of each organization are discussed.

Word of Wisdom (WoW): Found in Doctrine and Covenants 89, the Word of Wisdom is a specific summary of, or guideline for, what members of the Church should partake of with regard to food and drink. The Word of Wisdom also contains the specific blessings available to those who obey this commandment.

Young Men (YM): The organization within the Church designed for young men between the ages of twelve and eighteen years.

young single adults (YSA): The program in the Church designed for unmarried members of the Church, ages eighteen through thirty.

Young Women (YW): Similar to the Young Men organization, this program is designed for young women in the Church between the ages of twelve and eighteen years.

Zion: A word found in LDS culture that has several meanings. Literally the word means "the pure in heart." It can also refer to a specific location where the righteous are gathered together. It is often also used to refer to the membership of the Church as a whole.

Wow, that was some list! I congratulate any of you who have managed to keep reading long enough to get to the end! I was actually tempted to put in a couple of nonsense words just to see if you were paying attention, but since this language of Mormonism is new to you, I figured that might not be a good idea. As I mentioned at the beginning of the chapter, this is in no way a complete list of words, phrases, and ideas you are bound to come across on your exciting journey as a new member of the Church. The best advice anyone could give to you is, ask! When someone says something you don't understand, ask him to explain what he meant. If you hear a word in a meeting that you're unfamiliar with, ask someone to clarify it for you. I can tell you that no one will be offended and no one will think that you're a bit short in the brains department—it's just that many of us have been around these words and phrases so long that they're second nature to us and we don't stop for a second to realize that there may be someone listening who is new to the language.

NOTES

1. Gordon B. Hinckley, "'In . . . Counsellors There Is Safety'," *Ensign*, Nov. 1990, 48.
2. "History of BYU," Brigham Young University, accessed Dec. 30, 2009, http://yfacts.byu.edu/viewarticle.aspx?id=137.
3. Henry B. Eyring, "Rise to Your Call," *Ensign*, Nov. 2002, 75.
4. *Wikipedia*, s.v. "Church Educational System," accessed Dec. 31, 2009, http://en.wikipedia.org/wiki/Church_Educational_System.
5. "EFY Youth Programs," Brigham Young University, accessed Dec. 31, 2009, http://ce.byu.edu/yp/efy/.
6. "Introduction to Primary," The Church of Jesus Christ of Latter-day Saints, accessed Dec. 31, 2009, http://www.lds.org/pa/display/0,17884,4695-1,00.html.
7. "Relief Society," The Church of Jesus Christ of Latter-day Saints, accessed

Dec. 31, 2009, http://lds.org/ldsorg/v/index.jsp?index=18&locale=0&sourceId=4f519c57af139010VgnVCM1000004d82620a____&vgnextoid=bbd508f54922d010VgnVCM1000004d82620aRCRD.

8. D. Todd Christofferson, "A Sense of the Sacred," *New Era*, June 2006, 28–31.

About the Author

Carmen Davis was born in a small town in rural British Columbia, Canada, the second of eight children born to Dennis and Mae Dilts—the best parents anyone could be lucky enough to have. Her childhood memories almost all include some crazy adventure or another.

After graduating from high school in Fernie, BC, she attended Ricks College in Rexburg, Idaho, where she made many wonderful memories with the help of some incredible roommates and great friends, particularly from the baseball team. The many days sitting in the rain and cold in Idaho helped add to her love of all things baseball.

Upon graduating from Ricks, she took a brief journey north to attend the University of Lethbridge, which she quickly discovered was not for her, and by October of that fall, she had received her admissions letter to Brigham Young University in Provo, Utah. She graduated from BYU with a degree in political science, a major she loved but has found difficult to pursue in the rural areas she has lived.

In 1992 she met and fell in love with her husband, Shan. They were married in Las Vegas in April 1993 and sealed in the temple five years later after Shan joined the church. They have been blessed with four wonderful, healthy, baseball-playing boys who are the light of her life.

Carmen currently lives in Eureka, Montana, a very small town near the Canadian border, where she substitutes in the school district and volunteers in her boys' many endeavors.

She has served in various areas of the Church: multiple times as Primary secretary and as Young Women president, Relief Society teacher, Faith in God leader, Relief Society secretary, and currently in what she feels is the best calling in the Church: young adult Sunday School teacher.